Miscarriage of Mer

British False Memory Society
Bradford on Avon Wiltshire BA15 1NF
www.bfms.org.uk
Registered Charity No. 1040683

)eset in Latin Modern using KOMA-Script and LyX for LATEX

ted and bound in the UK by Lightning Source

sh Library Cataloguing in Publication Data
available
J-13: 978-0-9555184-1-6

Miscarriage of Memory

Historic abuse cases — a dilemma for the legal system

Edited by
Norman Brand, William Burgoyne,
Madeline Greenhalgh and Donna Kelly

BFMS

T
Pr
Br
Da
ISE

This book is dedicated to:

Roger Scotford who created the British False Memory Society, thus providing a place of comfort and answers for parents and others who have been falsely accused, and a focus for academic debate on the contentious issue of memory.

All families broken by false memories, in the hope that this book will help them to be reunited.

Miscarriage of Memory

A factual account of some of the injustices and accompanying family tragedies that have arisen when prosecution evidence is based on 'memories' allegedly recovered by complainants while undergoing psychotherapy or coming under other authoritative influences described in this book.

Most of the examples related in the following pages have been drawn from several thousand case histories reported to the British False Memory Society (BFMS). Of this number there were, at the time of publication, at least 672 cases where there is known to have been involvement by the police or a higher legal authority.

Miscarriage of Memory is a companion book to *Fractured families [Brand, 2007]*. Several case histories featured in *Fractured families* where the legal authorities were involved have been updated by the contributors and appear in Part IV of this book.

The work of the BFMS is supported by an autonomous Scientific and Professional Advisory Board comprising some of the most respected names in psychiatry, psychology and related disciplines. The Board provides the BFMS with guidance and advice concerning scientific, legal and professional enquiry into all aspects of false accusations of abuse. Whilst members of the board support the purposes of BFMS, the views expressed in this book might not necessarily be held by some or all of the board members. Likewise the views expressed in articles in this book are the authors' own and may not reflect those of the BFMS.

Scientific & Professional Advisory Board

Who is right — 'Bitter controversy' or 'Common sense'?

'Bitter controversy'

How trauma victims remember or forget their most horrific experiences lies at the heart of the most bitter controversy in psychology and psychiatry in recent times ... Arguably the most serious catastrophe since the lobotomy era ... Memory has become the flashpoint of one of the most bitter controversies ever to afflict the fields of psychology and psychiatry... How people remember or forget their most horrific experiences has become the central battleground of the memory wars.

'Debunking Myths about Trauma and Memory' [2005]
Richard J. McNally, Professor, Department of Psychology, Harvard University

We believe that what appear to be newly remembered (i.e. recovered) memories of past trauma are sometimes accurate, sometimes inaccurate, and sometimes a mixture of accuracy and inaccuracy; that much of what is recalled cannot be confirmed or disconfirmed; and that, because of these two beliefs, reports of past trauma based on such recovered memories are not reliable enough to be the sole basis for legal decisions.

'Recovered and False Memories' [2006a]
Dr Daniel B. Wright, Reader of Psychology, University of Sussex, Dr James Ost, Senior Lecturer in Psychology, International Centre for Research in Forensic Psychology, University of Portsmouth, Professor Christopher C. French, Professor of Psychology Goldsmiths College, University of London

For a longer version 'Ten years after — what we know now that we didn't know then about recovered and false memories' see Wright et al. [2006b].

> We now ... have hundreds of cases of wrongful convictions. People who have spent five and ten and fifteen or more years in prison for crimes they didn't do.

Professor Elizabeth Loftus, Professor of Law, University of California, Irvine, USA (advisor to 'The Memory and the Law Committee,' a working party of the Research Board of the British Psychological Society), speaking on 'Can You Trust Your Memory', BBC Radio 4, *Law in Action*, 17 June 2008.

Or 'Common sense'?

> Essentially the professor's evidence of the results of research into memories goes little further than is common sense and well within the normal human experience.

Comment made in the 2006 ruling by the Court of Appeal — *R* v *Bowman* [2006] EWCA Crim 417 (02 March 2006), paragraph 168 — that expert witness evidence on memory should not be allowed as a ground for appeal by Thomas Bowman against his conviction for murdering his wife in 1978. The trial was, initially, based on 'memories' of the event allegedly forgotten but recovered in great detail by his daughter while undergoing counselling twenty years later at the age of 26. A full report is given in chapter 22.

> "I think, frankly, that is a faintly ridiculous suggestion (referring to the use of memory expert witnesses in court cases). We do have experts who can be very helpful ... there are handwriting experts, there are fingerprint experts, and of course there are the DNA experts who have turned out to be of immense value in the courts. But we also have juries who are there in order to use their common sense and when it is a situation that you weigh up a witness's evidence and decide whether he or she is telling the truth or that he or she has a faithful recollection of what has taken place, this is essentially a matter for the jury. It is not a matter for an expert.

Retired Judge Gerald Butler, when asked whether we had reached the stage in this country where we needed memory experts to come and explain to juries how people's memories work, speaking on 'Can You Trust Your Memory', BBC Radio 4, *Law in Action*, 17 June 2008.

Contents

All names and places mentioned in the families' accounts have been changed to protect privacy with the exception of those which are already in the public domain. Where pseudonyms are used any similarity to the name of a real person is coincidental and unintended.

Acknowledgements

The editors would like to thank all who have contributed to this book: parents, grandparents, uncles, siblings and other adults whose experiences of being falsely accused are related in Parts IV, V and VI; those accusers who have recognised the falsity of their accusations — without their courage in telling their stories Part I of this book would not have been possible. Also we thank a psychiatrist, psychologists and legal professionals for their valuable contributions, comments and advice.

Conceived by William Burgoyne as a companion book to *Fractured families* and compiled and edited by

Norman Brand, Editor, *Fractured families*
William Burgoyne, Author, *Counselling or quackery?*
Madeline Greenhalgh, Director, BFMS
Donna Kelly, Technical Adviser

Foreword

The Right Hon. The Earl Howe, Parliamentary Under Secretary of State, Department of Health, and formerly Vice-Chair of the All-Party Parliamentary Group for Abuse Investigations

The phenomenon of false memory first came to my attention some years ago when I received a letter from a mother who asked me to meet her, and the story she told me was truly appalling. She and her husband were professional people with three grown-up children. The youngest was a 17 year old daughter who had received counselling for depression and then, suddenly, stopped talking to her parents.

When she did start talking to them the things she said totally shattered the family. She maintained she had been able to remember, in considerable detail, being repeatedly sexually abused by her father from about the age of four, these memories having been locked away and completely forgotten until she entered counselling.

The father was adamant that never in his life would he have done the things he was being accused of. Later, when the specific dates and times were looked at, it was quite clear that it would have been impossible for many to have taken place.

Thus it was that, having been alerted to the question of whether therapies may exert a harmful power on the mind, particularly of those who are already vulnerable, I raised the matter in the House of Lords (Lords Hansard 17 October 2001, column 645 *et seq*).

This book traces the effects which the theory of recovered memory has had: on our legal processes, civil and criminal; at the sway it has held over professional bodies and looks at its spread across the globe. It evokes a glimmer, perhaps no more, of the damage done to loving and united families.

Five years ago, as Opposition Health spokesman in the House of Lords and Deputy Chairman of the all-party committee on abuse investigations, I was invited to address the Annual General Meeting of the British False Memory Society. I was happy to see this as an opportunity to call for more openness and scepticism in the legal system and social services when dealing with abuse allegations.

It was the issue of memories of childhood abuse, allegedly recovered by adults who had no prior knowledge of the abuse until undergoing therapy — that decided me to accept the invitation.

My audience of 100, mostly parents and grandparents, had one thing in common: they had all been accused of child abuse. Some had been arrested, others were acquitted in court, a few were found guilty and imprisoned.

Others had been released on appeal or had served their sentence and were seeking to prove their innocence. Some of their stories are told here.

As for the family whose story began this foreword, the young woman continued to elaborate her account and claimed to have 'remembered' — again while undergoing therapy — being sexually assaulted by her brother. This was alleged to have happened at a time when she shared a room with her sister who asserted vehemently that nothing wrong had ever taken place.

This story echoes similar ones that I have since received from other families. Where such statements cannot be easily disproved, as in the above case, the police and social services are drawn in. The accused — usually, but not always, a father — may find himself involved in a desperate attempt to disprove allegations reaching back 20 or 30 years.

Childhood medical and school records may have been destroyed and there may be little more evidence to use in defence other than character references and the accused's word that nothing of the sort happened. It is these cases — 672 known to the BFMS where legal enquiries followed — that underline the need for this book, *Miscarriage of Memory*.

In describing in my Lords speech how false allegations can arise, I said:

> If there was one overriding observation I could make about any of the phenomena associated with wrongful allegations ... it is the extraordinary absence of scepticism which has allowed those phenomena to flourish and gain public acceptance.

I underlined that message in 2007 at the launch of the BFMS book, *Fractured families*, by saying:

> There is a general lack of awareness about the whole problem. Indeed many cases are still occurring that are characterised ... by an uncritical acceptance by police and social workers about newly remembered abuse. And what tends to happen is that the system just closes up.

The need for the BFMS to publish a book such as *Miscarriage of Memory* is itself evidence that injustices caused by a lack of understanding of memory throughout the legal system continue.

I congratulate the Society on having produced this book, *Miscarriage of Memory*, and commend it as standard reading for all who are interested in maintaining the highest levels of justice within the legal system.

Introduction

Madeline Greenhalgh, Director, British False Memory Society

Miscarriage of Memory is the second book to be published by the BFMS. In the first book, *Fractured families*, we highlighted the suffering of the families and individuals caught up in the fall out from false memories which have led to false accusations of a criminal nature. As we learned there, the effects are far reaching and go beyond the sadness and loss associated with family breakdown. In this book we take a look in greater detail at some of those effects. Devastating too is the level of injustice faced by those who are falsely accused of the heinous crime of historic child sexual abuse. We are not talking here of the horrors of contemporaneous claims of rape as in date rape or stranger rape but of claims of crimes alleged to have occurred years ago, sometimes several decades ago which are vehemently denied. These are cases where what evidence could be used may be long gone, as witnesses from the years in question may have died and any records pertaining to the time destroyed or lost.

Of course, repercussions from being falsely accused are not limited to facing a criminal investigation. Hand in hand with an accusation it is claimed that there can be 'no smoke without fire'. 'Why,' it is asked, 'would anyone reveal horrendous accounts of sexual abuse if there is no truth in them?' The key to understanding these cases is in recognising the peculiarities of accusations which have arisen with no prior knowledge of the events, perhaps during therapy or through some similar authoritative process. *Miscarriage of Memory* is an important step in helping anyone involved in their day-to-day work with child protection to understand how important it is to assess each case thoroughly on the facts. It is something peculiar to a sexual abuse case that makes it abhorrent, in the eyes of the public, that any hint of doubt should be cast or challenging questions raised about it.

This is understandable in view of the nature of the alleged crime but we cannot suspend all common sense; to do so will help no one. It is barbaric that the nature of an accusation should be seen as sufficient to condemn. We live in a civilised world, in a democracy where there is an expectation of justice for all. That is, however, unless you are falsely accused of sexual abuse. Your credibility and standing in your community are wiped out; you can be sacked from your job and find it impossible to obtain another one once your Criminal Records Bureau check is tainted with the charges; your future relationships and right to family life can be denied you and social services, all powerful in these scenarios, can ensure that you are excluded from your home. Under these circumstances, surely it is inhuman to deny an innocent person a voice.

During the past decade there has been much progress in the quality of the scientific research now available about the way that memory operates and the potential that exists for false memories to occur. Expert evidence, although frowned upon by some judges in these cases, is necessary to help jury members understand the complex nature of memory confabulation and misattribution, childhood amnesia and the unreliability of memory in general, but in particular, in young children. Also, knowledge of the effects of suggestibility, the effects of authoritative pressure and interview bias are not generally understood by the average lay person who may be called to jury service.

To improve this state of affairs for the future we need to continue to provide a voice for the minority of people falsely accused of historic sexual abuse. *Miscarriage of Memory* is necessary as part of that commitment to raising their profile thus helping to educate the public and professionals so that without exception a thorough investigation of the facts must be completed before condemning too readily. This nightmare, for that is how it is described by people who are innocent and caught up in it, can destroy a life; can strike anyone, anywhere and at anytime.

But there is life after false accusation; it is not easy but many have managed it. A few have rebuilt their families. None achieved it by doing nothing, by simply relying on their belief that justice will prevail. They had to work hard at it and to garner all the help they could from their friends and families, their legal teams and the BFMS. We need to keep the fear surrounding this issue in perspective by improving the education of professionals, raising awareness of the issues for the general public and ensuring a fair hearing for individuals who are falsely accused.

Content notes

William Burgoyne, author, Counselling or Quackery?

Some of the worst miscarriages in the history of the justice system have arisen directly out of a lack of understanding of memory, particularly childhood memory, by judges, juries and prosecution and defence counsels.

A selection of such miscarriages — and cases where there was initial police or Crown Prosecution Service (CPS) involvement but no further action[1] — is given in this book. In these cases an adult or older child, while undergoing psychotherapy or after reading potentially damaging self-help books such as *The courage to heal* [Bass and Davis, 1988],[2] came to believe that they had been able to uncover a previously unknown history of abuse in early childhood. Of the cases recorded by the BFMS, 672 — about one-quarter of the total — have involved some level of criminal investigation. This is undoubtedly an understatement as victims of false memory allegations may not seek help, or may go to other organisations for support.

The generally understood definition of a miscarriage of justice is where 'an innocent person is convicted of a crime.' For the purpose of this book, however, it includes cases which did not result in a guilty verdict. For even where enquiries went no further than an initial police investigation, accompanied by a dawn raid by teams of police and social workers, followed by detention in custody for questioning and widespread publicity, the outcome is a life sentence for all involved, as the cases in Part IV demonstrate.

Of those cases that did not fall after an initial police investigation, some went as far as Crown Court before being rejected at the pre-trial hearing or by the jury at trial. In a number, the defendants were found guilty and given long prison sentences before being released on appeal. In cases where a guilty verdict was returned and not overturned on appeal, the accused are still fighting for justice after serving their sentence or from within prison or, as in a few cases, a relative is seeking posthumous justice. The most recent cases are not included; they are either *sub judice* or subject to the restrictions of the family courts. The BFMS is continually assisting defendants accused of abuse on the basis of 'memories' allegedly recovered by adults undergoing therapy.

The phrase 'miscarriage of memory' is defined here as also including injustices caused by the failure of the British legal system to provide any redress for third parties against the accuser's therapist. Under English and Scottish laws, practitioners owe no duty of care to third parties; their responsibility is solely to the patient directly under their care — unlike the USA where successful and expensive law suits have dissuaded medical insurance companies from providing cover for practitioners of recovered memory therapies,[3] resulting in a considerable reduction in the number of false allegations cases. This anomaly is perfectly illustrated by the ruling of the Scottish court on liability for the foreseeable consequences of therapy on third parties in the Fairlie case (chapter 31). At the moment it seems that the only way that redress can be obtained under the legal system is for the accused to sue the accuser (usually a family member and clearly not a realistic option), and for the accuser then to sue the psychotherapist.

This single UK case where third party liability was tested in court is included in order to highlight the failure of UK courts to consider guidance given in a report commissioned by the Royal College of Psychiatrists (RCP)[4] that practitioners do, in fact, owe a duty of care to third parties. Although this report was relegated to the level of a discussion document published in the *British Journal of Psychiatry* in 1998, the college did issue a set of recommendations [Royal College of Psychiatrists' Working Group on Reported Recovered Memories of Child Sexual Abuse, 1997] approved by the College which stated:

> The welfare of the patient is the first concern of the psychiatrist. Concern for the needs of the family members and others may also be necessary, within the constraints imposed by the need for confidentiality.

Several cases heard by the General Medical Council (GMC) and the British Psychological Society (BPS) under their disciplinary procedures are included.[5] Cases such as those featured in Part IV have made psychiatrists and psychologists cautious when presented with 'memories' that the patient appears to have recovered during treatment. As retired Consultant Clinical Psychologist Katharine Mair says in chapter 6:

> My impression is that clinical psychologists working in the NHS are now more aware of the dangers of prompting false memories, and are far less likely to diagnose DID [dissociative identity disorder] or to discover ritual abuse. Sadly, however, there is now a growing band of independent, unregulated therapists who work privately are unlikely ever to see any guidelines.

The Health Professions Council position statement on the regulation of psychotherapists and counsellors states:

> At the moment, a psychotherapist or counsellor who is removed from the membership of their professional body for any reason

can simply continue in practice without there being any legal means for preventing potential harm to members of the public [Health Professions Council, 2009c].

However, this is likely to change following the decision announced by the Health Professions Council in December 2009 that it will recommend to the government that psychotherapists and counsellors should come within its regulatory system. A summary of the HPC's proposals is given in chapter 8. The earliest that these proposals can be implemented is 2011 [Health Professions Council, 2009a].

Thus, misconduct by therapists and counsellors is not at the moment recorded in the same way as by the GMC and BPS. In reading the following, a distorted impression may therefore be given that the problem lies largely with psychiatrists and psychologists. In fact, from the database of several thousand cases held by the BFMS, most cases arise from treatment by counsellors and therapists.

No document purporting to cover the subject of false memory would be complete without reference to religious cults where recovered memory practices form part of their initiation procedures. While cults have often been featured in the national press, there has been little or no publicity for this aspect of their activities. Yet cases known to the BFMS show that they can be no less damaging — perhaps more so — than cases arising from psychotherapy. In her report on the situation in the United States Pamela Freyd, Executive Director of the False Memory Syndrome Foundation of America, says:

> Unfortunately, there are still minimally trained people who don't understand. Many of these people practice under the auspices of religious counselling and are thus immune from any state controls [Freyd, 2007].

Unfortunately, the continuing practice of regression therapy within a religious context in the USA has consequences far beyond its shores. The BFMS has on its files a number of cases where adult children of British parents have been subjected to regression therapies as part of initiation ceremonies prior to acceptance by cults, with tragic consequences.

Much of what follows refers to the effects on parents who are falsely accused by an adult son or daughter. However the experiences described are no less traumatic where the accusations are made against a sibling, other family members, a family friend, neighbour, teacher, social worker or voluntary worker.

It is essential, in any consideration of the consequences of false memories, not to ignore the effect on the accuser, particularly when he or she recognises the falsity of the allegations.[6] As the 'Brandon' report says,

> The damage done to families if the accusation is untrue is immense. Moreover, it is not only families that are damaged by mistakes in this area. Patients who are mistakenly diagnosed as having been abused frequently end as mental health casualties [Brandon et al., 1998].

This consequence of false memories is painfully evident in the case histories related in Part I.

The justice system should not take the above concerns lightly. To be falsely accused of the most heinous crime of child abuse, and to have your name disclosed to the press and public, places defendants and their families on a level in society — and within the prison system — below that of murderers, even multiple murderers. In many cases known to the BFMS there is long term or permanent damage to the mental and/or physical health of the accused. Breakdown, severe depression and thoughts of suicide are not uncommon [Gudjonsson, 2006].

The immensity of the lifelong stigma attached to such accusations arising out of therapy demands a thorough review of investigative procedures including, in particular, the response of the police officer receiving the initial complaint. If therapy in any shape or form figures in the evidence, then expert opinion should be sought before making dawn raids on innocent, unsuspecting parents, as described in several of the case histories related in Part IV (the same point is made by barrister Pamela Radcliffe in chapter 10).

Although the purpose of this book is to highlight the pernicious effect of false, recovered memories within the justice system, the huge financial cost to the taxpayer and to the accused in financing his or her own defence should not be ignored. Accurate figures do not exist for the waste in terms of legal resources and public money. However, there is no doubt that this is considerable. In just one case a second trial of two defendants lasting four weeks that followed a family court hearing involved eight months of legal advice at a cost of over £1million. This did not include the cost of the full hearing in the Family Court and an appeal leading to the second hearing, or the waste of police resources, so the total cost will have been several times greater. The father in chapter 25 reports that the costs to him, personally, were £600,000. Social services wasted over £250,000 of taxpayers' money. The legal and police costs to the taxpayer would certainly have been several million pounds. Multiply these available figures by the number of cases known to the BFMS and it is likely that the total waste of public money in pursuing failed actions based on allegations arising from 'recovered' memories will not be far short of £1billion.

Part I.

Where it all starts: a vulnerable person seeks help — a fertile breeding ground for false memory

Introduction to Part I

Every problem has a starting point. In the case of false memory this is usually (but not exclusively) vulnerability — the vulnerability of the patient/client. Vulnerability provides the fertile ground for false memory to take root. The experiences of four 'retractors' tell how this can happen. The first, by 'Phoebe', is a verbatim transcript of a presentation she gave at the 2008 AGM of the BFMS. Later, it was printed and sent to every child and adolescent mental health unit in Britain. The second, by 'Holly,' is the full text of the legally witnessed statement by an accusing daughter whose parents' experiences are related in chapter 27. The third is taken from the October 2005 Newsletter of the BFMS and is told by Dr Peter Naish, Senior Lecturer in Psychology, The Open University and Chairman of the BFMS Scientific and Professional Advisory Board. The fourth comes from the USA — where the false memory movement originated. The author has only now felt able to write of her experiences and in 2009 sent her story to the BFMS Internet forum to help other retractors deal with their long-term feelings of guilt.

All are written under pseudonyms. A further selection of retractors' stories may be read in various editions of the Newsletter, available on the BFMS website at www.bfms.org.uk.

Retractors' stories, by their very nature, relate to false accusations made, often, many years beforehand. But this passage of time does not affect their relevance to the debate on false memory today — rather it highlights the long-term damage caused to the falsely accused and the even longer (sometimes lifelong) sense of guilt experienced by retractors when they recognise the harm caused, even though the fault is not theirs.

'Hope'

To my accusing daughter I would say: 'Don't let remorse ruin what will be left of your life.' And I absolutely mean it. Somebody, some cult or fashion got at her, sensed an opportunity and pounced. Over the many years since I last saw her she will have built a new life. How can she tear such an edifice down?

I write this because I hope that at some time, maybe many years ahead, there will be a person who pulls a 'trigger' in time which will destroy the fallacy of false 'memory'. Who would have thought that the Berlin Wall would come down? It just happened.

It seems that the stalemate goes on for ever: year after year after year.

Parents like me have come to live with a living bereavement. We still go on holiday, pay the newspaper bill, chat with the neighbours.

But 'for ever' ends. I die. Other loved ones die. Therapists or cultists, from mixed motives or perhaps genuine troubles or convictions of their own, have planted the idea of parental abuse in childhood into vulnerable adults.

We hope for a fair hearing from politicians, social workers, lawyers, doctors etc. — and fight for it on that level. Ultimately, however, this goes deeper than all that. It's about reconciliation. I will not accept that this is impossible.

An accused father

(BFMS Forum 2009)

1. Phoebe's story: 'Behind closed doors': struggling to stay alive in a child and adolescent mental health unit

This document is the transcript of an address given by a young woman at the Annual General Meeting of the BFMS in 2008. She describes her teenage experiences in a child and adolescent mental health unit which led her to make false accusations of sexual abuse. She wants CAMH Units to be aware of the preventable dangers that arise from the type of treatment she received. With recent reports of absconding, attempted suicides and actual suicides occurring in adolescent units, her story presents a compelling reason for change.

Childhood

I am the oldest of three children. I had a very happy, unremarkable childhood. I was unusually tall as a child and a specialist predicted I would be 6' 3" by adulthood. My parents felt I would not be able to cope with the social complexities of being a very tall woman, and I had hormone treatment at the age of 9 which induced early puberty with the goal of limiting my final height. At 11 I went to boarding school. I had experienced the hormone treatment itself as quite invasive, and its effects left me ill-equipped to deal with boarding school's tough communal living.

In retrospect, I would say that by the age of 12 I was clearly clinically depressed. Throughout adolescence and adulthood I have suffered from recurrent depressive episodes which have not been precipitated by any particular external events. During these episodes I suffer significant insomnia, loss of appetite and nausea, flatness and despair. My poor eating was picked up by the school and I saw an eating disorder specialist. The sessions did not help me and she referred me to a child and adolescent psychiatrist in the area of my boarding school. In her referral letter, she said:

P reveals very little to me and is obviously very loyal and wary of change. P is extremely conscientious, sensitive to other people's feelings and wanting to please.

Initial outpatient sessions with the psychiatrist

The sessions with the new psychiatrist did not go much better. Though his early letters and notes are littered with references to depression, I do not remember anyone ever telling me this diagnosis, or what it meant. Nobody said to me: you are not the first person in the world to feel like this. The way you are feeling now is a recognised condition. When people feel like this they sit tight and wait it out. Because I did not know what depression was, or that I had it, I was frightened and desperate. I was also vulnerable to the suggestion that the onus was on me to explain why I was feeling like this. I had experienced some significant life events. A close family friend had died. There was the hormone treatment and its effects. I had difficulties in my relationship with my sister. I was experiencing the usual teenage struggles with my parents. I was acutely aware, however, that they did not account for how I was feeling. Neither did they appear to be sufficient explanations for the psychiatrist, who wrote to my doctor:

> there are probably other factors of relevance in P's history, but at this stage it is hard to be clear what they are.

Because the psychiatrist's notes do not include his side of the conversation regarding how he responded to the problems I did reveal, or how he approached determining these 'other factors', I can only say how I felt. I felt that he believed that my difficulties were caused by some significant life event, which he believed I was concealing. I felt under pressure to account for the depth of my unhappiness, and that the real problems I did offer up were not considered sufficient. I remember lying awake the nights before the sessions, wondering what I would be able to offer the next day. Beyond this, I also began to believe myself that there must be One Big Reason why I was feeling so awful, and my failure to find one only added to my panic and despair.

Beyond mentioning these everyday problems, which I did spontaneously and without a high degree of specific questioning, I was largely silent. To be fair, I was giving indications in those early days that there were things I could not talk about. I was desperately struggling — and utterly failing — to deal with the fact that I was gay. It was causing me great distress, but I did not feel able to talk to the psychiatrist or anyone else about it. At the General Medical Council [a GMC hearing brought by P's parents against her psychiatrist], these indications that I had something more to talk about were used as justification for the psychiatrist's belief that something else significant had happened to me.

The psychiatrist decided I would benefit from antidepressants. I believe we discussed that the tablets were dangerous in overdose, though I can find no record of this discussion. I had direct access to the tablets and, feeling increasingly desperate, I took too many. I was admitted to the paediatric ward of the nearest hospital and then to the psychiatrist's adolescent unit on the same site.

First impressions of Unit

It is difficult to describe the shock of the exposure to the world of the Unit. It was like nothing I could ever have imagined. All the rules of the normal world were suddenly turned on their head. Everyone was intent on injuring or killing themselves, while staff tried half-heartedly to stop them. I saw a patient with terrible scarring to her arms on my first day there, and my first thought was to wonder who had done that to her, when it dawned on me that she had done it to herself. I began self-harming very quickly — it made perfect sense in that environment, which was so restricted that all the normal healthy coping strategies were unavailable. I was able to secretly obtain razor blades from other patients who had brought them onto the unit. It was a strange environment in which problems became infectious and everyone's misery fed off everyone else's. At lunch that first day, having always been a fussy eater, I couldn't eat the food. I remember a particularly aggressive member of staff accusing me of having an eating disorder. I couldn't reply. I was blinking back the tears thinking 'no, I just don't eat this; ask my mum, she'll tell you.' And I was hit with the realisation that my mother wasn't there, and that not even she could help me now.

I was by far the youngest patient and I was out of my depth. I understand that 'trauma' is a loaded word, but I do not think it is an overstatement to say that I was traumatised by my sudden submersion into inpatient psychiatric care, at a time when I was at my lowest and most vulnerable and had no resources to draw on. A different psychiatrist reported seeing me smile for the first time six weeks after my admission.

Again, because there are no records of the general attitude on the unit, I can only talk about how I personally perceived it. I felt there was a strong message which said: you can't leave here until you're better. We can't help you get better unless we know what's wrong. You must give us a reason for why you're feeling like this. A nursing note from early in my admission recorded:

Very tearful. No explanations. Answering direct questioning.

That is how it started. I had no explanations to offer.

First allegations and response

I was deteriorating. In the days leading up to the allegations I was seeing the psychiatrist at least once a day. I had been in the unit a few weeks by then. There were two sessions the day the first allegations emerged. When I looked at my medical records I was surprised by how easy it is to see how the allegations arose, and I share that now ...

> P very withdrawn — not talking. I talked about her discussion that it felt that there were people who had let her down, people who had made promises to her who had somehow or other then gone away. Reminded P she said there were more people. I asked P how many other people. She said one. I asked whether adult or child and after a lot of hesitation P said — adult. Male or female? Again after a lot of hesitation P said male, in a whisper. Was it family? No it wasn't. Was it someone P had known a long time? No it wasn't. Was it somebody in the country? No it wasn't. Was it somebody at her primary school? No. Was it someone at her secondary school? No. Was it someone in London? Silence. I suggested to P that I guessed that it sounded as if it was somebody in London. Given that it was neither family nor school and it was clearly somebody else, I wondered if perhaps it was somebody medical. P agreed that it was. I asked whether 'it' had happened once or on a number of occasions. P said it happened on a number of occasions. I wondered where, given that it was a male doctor. I'm aware that P has only seen one male doctor. P agreed this is the case. I asked P when she first saw the doctor. P said when she was 8. I then asked P when she first felt uncomfortable. P said when she was 9. P declined to talk further about what had happened. I suggested to P that I see her again shortly to talk about it further.

The psychiatrist clearly determined the agenda that day. Me 'being let down' became 'it' which became me 'feeling uncomfortable'. As far as I remember, I did not know what we were talking about. Where a question had two possible outcomes, I hesitantly selected one. When a question could be simply answered 'no', I did so. When we ran out of options, I said nothing. This was taken as a 'yes'.

I am at a loss to explain what happened that afternoon, because the entire afternoon session is described in five lines and a few words and this is how they begin ...

> In this session P moved on to talk about how ... [and then allegations of sexual abuse] ...

I do not know whether I made those allegations spontaneously or in the context of a question and answer session similar to that which had taken place earlier in the day. It was not pre-meditated. I have no idea what I was thinking. I had not planned to talk about the hormone treatment that day. I had not in fact known that the psychiatrist had known about it. The psychiatrist reported at the GMC that he had expected me to tell him how very uncomfortable I felt because of the appropriate [hormone treatment] examination. Yet in a summary of key events prepared by the nurse manager for the police, it was reported that in a session eight days previously the psychiatrist had 'felt I was preparing to make a disclosure.' At the GMC the psychiatrist was asked: 'did you show your approval any way to the extent that now perhaps you were getting somewhere with her, that you were able to move on with her, that sort of thing?' He replied, 'I have little doubt that where [she] was able to speak, she got some sense of, well done, thank goodness you are talking.' In the weeks following the allegation the clinical staff noted I would not be judged Gillick competent[1] at this point.

Second allegations and context

One aspect of the unit I found particularly extraordinary was the way in which patients were treated as if they were a serious risk to themselves during the week, but were expected to go home and function normally at weekends. In the course of the weeks in the unit I had contracted an interest in self harm and suicide which left me feeling in serious danger of myself. It was a Friday, I was due to go home, and I was terrified that I wouldn't come back alive. I did not think this risk would be taken seriously (though later indications suggest that it may have been). I knew that I would be taken seriously if I said I was at risk from somebody else. I said my father had sexually abused me. These allegations, and all subsequent ones, were made to a member of the nursing staff who was giving me 'psychotherapy.' It wasn't calculation, it was desperation. I went to the children's ward for the weekend, as I would do every weekend for another year.

Final allegations

I went on to accuse two more men of abusing me. This happened in the context of a 'psychotherapy session.' The nurse asked a series of questions about the non-existent sexual abuse, things like how old was I when this first happened, and how many times had this happened, but then rather abruptly switched and asked if anyone else had done what my father had done. Again I felt that what I had already said wasn't enough and that they expected more. I was exhausted and worn down, and in desperation, I named the only two other adult males in my life, knowing that this was my final offer, because there simply weren't any other candidates.

Ongoing confusion/retractions

That same month, and throughout the next, I made a series of retractions — verbally and in writing — to unit staff, a social worker and my *guardian ad litem*. I said repeatedly that I wanted to go home and I set about trying to discharge myself. At the same time I continued to give details of the alleged abuse and twice retracted my retraction. I also at times said the reason I wanted to go home was so I would be free to commit suicide.

I also made an early attempt to indicate that the unit was making things worse, not better. One month after the initial allegations, the psychiatrist recorded:

> P said she felt in some ways we weren't helping her to survive but more helping her get into a mess.

He also records his response:

> I suggested that maybe the mess had been there at the outset and at least we knew now that she was in a mess.

By the next month, I had withdrawn from the staff at the unit. I had realised there was no straightforward way out of this mess, and the only way forward was to die. The next evening, I left the unit and attempted suicide. I didn't do it very well and I ended up back at the unit. I was in it deeper than ever.

In the next couple of months, my relationship with the unit changed dramatically. I stopped saying I wanted to go home, and became very afraid to leave. I was utterly institutionalised and dependent on them. With the increasing distance and difficulties with my family, I came to see my key-worker and the nurse-psychotherapist, and my intense friendships with fellow inpatients, as my family.

My mental and physical state

My mental and physical state seriously deteriorated during my time in the unit. I remained intermittently on sedative antidepressants. I was prescribed additional night sedation for long stretches, despite its highly addictive quality. The dosage was increased several times because I developed a tolerance to it. I was given an anti-psychotic drug when I was acutely distressed. I also had regular medication 'hang-overs.' But despite the highly sedative effects of all this medication, I slept little or not at all. I sustained extensive scarring to my arms, legs and torso over the year I was there. I was in constant pain from these wounds. My personal hygiene was very poor. I associated brushing my teeth with the 'abuse' I had suffered. I didn't wash or change my clothes because I was terrified of my own body. I stopped eating and drinking. By the psychiatrist's description, I was 'electively mute.' I felt suicidal for most of my time there. I truly believed that I would not leave the unit alive. From the point of view of the unit, my behaviour was difficult. I needed constant encouragement to take any fluids or food. I was not very compliant in taking my medication. I was able to abscond several times.

Attempted move and working relationships

After five months in the unit, my parents tried to move me to another unit. The pretext for this was that the current unit could not offer seven-day care, whereas the new unit would. Actually, they believed that if they could get me out from the influence of the current unit, the situation would right itself. My parents, social worker and guardian *ad litem* all agreed that the move was in my best interests. The psychiatrist opposed the move and, though it was decided on, it never happened. There are various records of the psychiatrist failing to forward my medical notes and requesting more time to treat me.

By this time I was aware of the very tense working relationships between the social services, the unit and my parents. The loyalty the eating disorder specialist had identified was still strong, but I had switched my allegiance to the unit. Because I had aligned myself firmly on the side of the unit, these tensions meant that I was further alienated from my parents, and I did not even trust my social worker enough to hold a conversation with her for many months. By now I was lying outright to, as I saw it, protect the unit. I said that I had self-harmed prior to coming into the unit, so that they would not be blamed for me picking up this habit. I said that I had told people about the abuse before I entered the unit, so that people could not blame them for 'planting the idea in my head.'

The tensions between the unit and all other parties are best captured in a memo from one social services manager to another, written, particularly poignantly, on my 14th birthday, some months after the attempted move. In it he said he felt that the psychiatrist wanted my parents' views disregarded. He believed that the psychiatrist saw himself as a continuing part of the investigative process and would not refer me to any other unit.

Continuing doubts and questions

Meanwhile, I continued to express my doubts about the abuse. Instead of retracting the allegations outright as in those first months, I began to ask questions. It was not that I was afraid of losing face, or that I felt that the legal and child protection processes had taken things out of my hands. I've already shown you that I was able to tell these people that the allegations were false. My dilemma was that I simply could not see why it would have arisen if it was not true, so I always fell back to the position that it must be true. I discussed this dilemma openly with the psychiatrist and unit staff, but did not get any satisfactory answers.

As time went on, the allegations became more and more part of my identity. I was identified by the staff and all the other patients as a victim of abuse. In my own head, fiction merged with reality and a fog of confusion descended. The list of symptoms for survivors of abuse is so wide that of course I displayed a number of genuine 'symptoms'. I also developed others, became intensely afraid of men and feared my father coming to find me. I had bad dreams in which awful stuff did happen to me (probably because the whole thing was so on my mind). And as I repeatedly encoded and retrieved the things I had made up, they effectively became memories. Beyond that, the theory of sexual abuse had explanatory power — it made sense of things otherwise unexplained — and I fell for that.

External process and feelings about it

In the background of all this, there was a powerful external process involving child protection investigations and care proceedings, and it deeply affected me. My future was terribly uncertain and after two Emergency Protection Orders and a rejected application for an interim Care Order, stalemate was reached. A Care Order was finally granted 11 months after my admission to the unit on the grounds that I was 'beyond parental control.' For the order to be granted, my parents had to concede that 'the role played by each member of the family may have contributed to the reactive condition that P now exhibits.'

About a month before I was discharged, the psychiatrist noted:

> P was at the most depressed I have seen her for some time, crying and saying 'I want to go home, I just want to go home' ... P said that her year with us had been even more awful than the abuse before.

And from a week later:

> Still saying she wants to go to London, wants to go home. When she tries to sleep main thought is 'I want my Mummy.' She desperately wants the abuse never to have happened.

Life in Care

I went into foster care. The only thing I knew was that I would rather die than ever go back to a place like the unit, so I threw everything into 'playing at real life'. I stopped self harming abruptly as soon as I left the unit. I resisted attempts by the unit to 'follow up' my care, refusing to be a day patient, missing appointments with the psychiatrist and making it difficult to schedule new ones. I did not follow-up the unit's referral to a local psychotherapist.

After the unit, I'd had enough drama to last me a lifetime. I went to school and made friends and did my homework. At first I was faking it but gradually I found that I was living. I didn't tell people in my new life that I had been abused, so I didn't lock myself into that identity. My mother visited and we would have a meal and chat about everyday things. Meanwhile, as time went on, the fog began to slowly lift. I developed stronger doubts and then a certainty in the pit of my stomach that the things I had said weren't true. I did not, however, really admit this even to myself. All my energy went into hanging onto the precarious life I had built for myself.

Sadly, my grandmother died while I was still estranged from my family. Before she died she wrote me a letter stating that she believed I was mistaken, and that her dearest wish was for me to rejoin my family. Though it was to take me another 14 months before I was able to do so, that letter did have an impact.

Some months into my time in care, my mother felt she could no longer go on visiting me and 'pretending' that everything was OK. She wanted me home, and it was all or nothing. We had no contact for many months. I missed my mother terribly, but I didn't feel I could go for the 'all' option, and, pushed to decide, I confirmed to my mother that I would never be coming home.

Coming home

Soon after doing so, I began to change my mind. I was grief-stricken at the idea of losing my family permanently, and I began to think with my social worker about how I might gradually go home. This in turn threatened the foster placement, and it was terminated by the foster carer with little warning. When my social worker began talking about approaching new foster placements, I knew that I wanted to go home. I had only ever really wanted to go home. Now that I had nowhere and no one to hide behind, it was surprisingly easy to ask if they would have me. Their response was an unequivocal 'yes, come home.' All credit to my family. Two and a half years had passed since I had entered the unit. I had had no contact at all with my father. I had had regular strained contact with my mother and infrequent contact with my siblings. I had not been into the city where we lived. Yet the day the school holidays began, I walked into our family home and we spent Christmas together. It really was that simple.

We had family therapy to talk in a controlled way about what had happened. My family were desperate for me to provide them with An Explanation for what had happened. I couldn't, because I didn't have one. I couldn't think about it or explain it even to myself. The family therapy gave them a way of letting me know what they had been through, which was desperately upsetting to hear. I did not reciprocate. If it was upsetting for me to learn how my parents had suffered, then how much more devastating would it be for a parent to learn of their child's suffering? Beyond my concern not to hurt my parents, I just had no words for what I'd experienced in the unit.

After the family therapy ended, we basically got on with it! We didn't rake over the past at breakfast, lunch and supper. In fact, we lived, largely, as if it had never happened. I am aware that cries of 'denial' will ensue from some quarters, but it wasn't like that. What I mean is that I re-entered my family on a totally equal footing. I was not held in debt, and I believe if I had been it would never have worked out.

I retracted the allegations to my family and to the social services, but I remained under a Care Order for another two years after I returned home. Three months before my 18th birthday, when the Care Order would have expired anyway, I applied to the court to have it lifted. It was a symbolic gesture.

Legalities since

My parents had long pursued a GMC case against the psychiatrist, which was finally heard in September 2003. The case centred around his handling of the initial allegations against the endocrinologist. It was found to be inappropriate and unprofessional that he told me he was 'worried he may have done it to other children' because 'it was likely to immediately strengthen my impression that I might have been inappropriately touched at the medical examination.' The psychiatrist himself admitted that the quality of his notes at the crucial period from the allegations ... was unsatisfactory ... and inadequate as a record of events. Frustratingly, his conduct could only be inferred based on his notes, but his defence offered several times that since 'the notes did not purport to be any more than an overall summary,' his conduct could not be established beyond doubt. Overall, it was decided, 'these limited failings seen in the light of his previously unblemished record could not amount to serious professional misconduct.' In his determination, the Chairman said:

> This case goes to the heart of a doctor's dilemma in circumstances when, whatever he does, criticism and controversy is likely to follow; situations in which there may be no absolute truth, no perfect answers ... The doctor has to have the courage of his convictions.

Notwithstanding their explanation that such convictions need to be based upon sound clinical evaluations and judgment, this determination horrifies me. It seems to me to do away entirely with reasonable standards of practice on the basis that we can't be perfect anyway. It seems to me to say: do what you like, as long as you believe hard enough in what you're doing.

I sued the psychiatrist, my key worker, the nurse who had administered the 'psychotherapy' and the nurse manager in 2004, a few weeks before the statute of limitations expired on my 21st birthday. The settlement negotiations centred around how much it might cost to have plastic surgery to repair the injuries I was able to inflict on myself during my time at the unit. In November 2004 the NHS Trust paid me £25,000 plus costs. They did not admit liability, but neither did they include a gagging clause.

My reason for telling my story

Sexual abuse is a very difficult subject. There continues to be a powerful voice which argues that allegations, especially from young people, are never false. As far as I can tell, the only way to establish that allegations can be untrue is if those who have made such allegations say so. So firstly, I want to say: I made allegations of sexual abuse which were utterly untrue. False allegations do happen.

Beyond that, I came here because I found out at the beginning of this year that things appear to remain largely unchanged at the adolescent unit in question. In 2004, five months before they settled my case, a sectioned patient was able to walk out of the unlocked door, with a noose around her neck from an earlier suicide attempt which staff had disrupted, and hanged herself from a tree in front of the unit. Her inquest heard that she was 'found with her arms in the branches as if she was trying to save herself.' I am devastated but not surprised. I feel it was only a matter of time before a patient died in their care. If I had tried a bit harder, I would have died in their care.

I have since discovered the existence of a group of former and current patients of the unit on a social networking site. I was appalled to see that young people who were only recently discharged are saying the very same things that my friends and I have said to each other about our time there in 1996. Although some of the comments are very positive about members of staff, they also say:

> I was always anxious that if I wasn't self harming/depressed or thin enough I would just be told to leave, even when at some level I wanted to stay because it felt like my only chance to 'get better.'

> It's not our illness we have survived, it's [the unit]!

Importantly, one of the expert witnesses called in the psychiatrist's defence at the GMC took issue with the idea that inpatient units are safe settings. He said, 'One is constantly concerned about the highly risky behaviour of young people in adolescent units and certainly I do not regard it as a safe place.' The other expert witness his defence called said: 'It is very interesting how very often when young people come in, they actually get worse when they are on the inpatient unit. You could ask why ...'

I'd like to make it really clear that I do not have a vendetta. I believe that what happened was bigger than one individual practitioner. I do think that the unit environment was a recipe for disaster. I think that what happened to me was one of the possible disastrous outcomes, but not the only one. Although it may be common knowledge among child and adolescent psychiatrists that adolescent units are not safe places, and that patients frequently deteriorate rather than improve, I do not think that it is widely understood by others. I know that my parents and I did not understand this prior to my admission. I wish we had.

How I have dealt with it

I'm going to explain now about how I have dealt with what happened. I have to admit that the 'dealing with it' has been very recent indeed. I was discharged from the unit 11 years ago this summer. Since I was discharged I have actively pushed away all thoughts and memories from that time. Last summer, there was something about the number '10' years ago that made me realise I had to understand what happened. This 'need to know' came on suddenly and took over everything.

It is difficult to describe the dilemma which cuts right to the heart of my sense of self. The question I have had to ask myself, and still ask often, is *how could this have happened to me?*

While I would agree with the assessment of the eating disorder specialist that I was conscientious and wanted badly to please, I would never have said that I am easily led. I'm not stupid. I have the top First in my year from Oxford, a distinction in my Masters degree and I am doing a PhD. During my time in the unit it was suggested by other parties that my intelligence might have enabled me to mastermind the whole operation. I can only assure you that I was in no state to mastermind anything, even my own suicide.

Much was also made at the GMC hearing of how at 13 I was angry, resentful and wilful. Though I know it may be difficult for you to judge, I hope that you can see that I have been honest enough about everything else to believe that, if I had made the allegations as a conscious act of will, a way to act out some resentment, I would say so here. I have sometimes believed that might be an easier truth to deal with: at least I would really know what happened. I could keep an eye on my temper and that would be that. Having said that, however, I do acknowledge that I was difficult, and I think it is unfortunate that the events I have described took place at a time when I was teenager anyway. I have found it somewhat difficult to unpick what was adolescence, what was personality, and what was illness.

As a person I have become much more circumspect, much more guarded. I take nothing on trust; instead I test everything out thoroughly myself. This makes me a good scientist but perhaps a slightly frustrating friend. Overall, I see these changes as positive: they are part of making sure that nothing similar ever happens again. Day to day, however, they do have a negative impact on my life. I struggle to trust other people, and am always alert for how their views might influence mine. I do not really trust myself to see things as they are, or to make the right decision, and so I avoid making commitments which cannot be reversed. Every day, to a greater or lesser extent, I struggle to find a way to live with myself and with what happened. Most days, I succeed. Crucial to this are the people who know all about me and love me just the same — my family, my partner and my friends. The bottom line for me is: I feel sure that if I had not been in that unit, I would not have made the allegations. Most days, that is enough to quiet my fears about myself.

Things that went right

Finally, I'm going to say a bit now about the things which went right. There was a happy ending because my family never let go. To me this was grace. There is a well known Biblical story of a son who leaves home, squanders his inheritance and returns only when he is destitute. Rather than resenting this, the father in the story sees his child when he is still far off, and comes to welcome him home. That is how my family welcomed me.

I had a fantastic social worker who was prepared to swim against the tide and make herself unpopular on all sides by saying that it was time to stop arguing about what had and hadn't happened, what was really imperative was to get me out of that unit before it was too late.

I had a lovely, small, nurturing school which took a huge chance on me, accepting me directly from full inpatient-status and allowing me to skip the year I had missed while in the unit.

I had a wonderful GP who was prepared to take sole medical responsibility for a patient with a formidable psychiatric history. I have not seen any kind of mental health professional since leaving the unit, and I never will.

When I moved to London, I moved back in with my parents. My mother and I have breakfast together most mornings, and this time together has allowed to us to make up for some of the time that we lost to the unit and my years in care. All our paths cross at home fairly often, but we treasure the times when we are 'all together as a family.' We treasure them perhaps more than most families, because we are so aware of how easily the ending could have been so different.

2. Holly's story: legally witnessed statement of retraction

I, HOLLY DAWSON of . . . make this statement believing it to be the honest truth as I now understand it.

I made a number of statements in the latter part of 1997 which at the time I genuinely believed to be true. I now wish to clarify the situation concerning the allegations of abuse which I made in September 1997 to various people including written statements made to the . . . Constabulary. The allegations which I made were specifically against my parents Mr and Mrs J Dawson of . . . and also my Aunt and Uncle Mr and Mrs E Dawson formerly of . . . On reflection I still cannot fully understand why I told so many malicious lies against those I love. In my own defence I can only say that it was so easy for me to slip into the role of a sexually abused person. Professionals had inferred that I had been sexually abused and that I displayed the majority of symptoms of a sexually abused person. It was just so easy for me to learn to think that way in order to fit in and to become a product of my institutionalised environments.

I was certainly aware of a traumatic personality change over a short period of time; for example, by nature I would not consider myself to be a malicious liar.

I feel that I could well have been a victim of what is now recognised as false memory syndrome and I feel that had I been treated differently by the system this situation may never have occurred.

There was never anything in my lifestyle that I can recall which could have resulted in the severe depression I was experiencing and for which I presumed I was being treated over a period-of seven years but unsuccessfully. I have never ever been sexually abused by anyone in my entire life and I now feel bitterly ashamed at the allegations I made against those who have loved me especially my parents who have stood by me in spite of everything.

In retrospect it seems a very small thing just to say I'm sorry when I consider the anguish and humiliation which was caused to innocent people. I feel totally ashamed of myself and ask my parents, Aunt[1] and others to try and forgive me for my part since I trust I have learnt a salutary lesson through my wrong doings.

---

[1]Holly's uncle had died before this statement was made

Dated this seventeenth day of June 1998

[The document is then signed and witnessed by two people including Holly's solicitor.] Holly adds the following by hand:

Mum and Dad
I hope this helps you
With much love in the Lord
Your daughter
Holly x

(See also chapter 27)

3. Louise's story: a story of real and false traumatic memories

This article, by Dr Peter Naish, Senior Lecturer in Psychology, The Open University and Chairman of the BFMS Scientific and Professional Advisory Board, was first published in the BFMS Newsletter, October 2005.

It was not long ago that I first met Louise; she had plucked up the courage to try hypnosis with me. Like many people, she was not entirely sure what hypnosis comprised, but had a general sense of unease about the whole thing. 'It didn't help that you were a bloke,' she later told me. However, she had been in touch with the BFMS Director, Madeline Greenhalgh, who had kindly indicated that I was to be trusted. I had been told only a little about Louise, but knew that she had been troubled by 'memories' which she felt must be false.

Few people carry their troubles openly and, like so many others, Louise was cheerful, almost bubbly; the tears came later. I subsequently learned that she was hoping to complete a degree course, and perhaps the label 'student-like' summed her up quite well. With the initial pleasantries over, we settled down to more formal ice-breaking, during which I could get to know a little more about her background. We then moved on to hypnosis, when a good deal of additional information emerged. I hasten to point out that this information was not elicited because the hypnosis magically accessed hidden memories! It is simply that being hypnotised generally engenders a sense of calm security, during which people feel able to address troubling material. Not all of the story I am about to tell was given to me that day; I have stayed in touch with Louise, and with her permission have filled the gaps, so that I can present the salient facts, in a sensible sequence.

They say that troubles, like buses, never come singly; I have certainly observed that current traumas seem often to afflict those who have become more susceptible, as it were, due to problems in the past. Again, I have to stress that this observation has nothing to do with seeking for 'repressed' material, as an explanation for present troubles; it is simply sensible to find anything that a person believes might still be contributing to their overall sense of unhappiness. With Louise it was a rape.

> I was really surprised how quickly you moved on from the 'memories' and had me talking about what happened. I had never told people all the details before, and it certainly hadn't been treated as an issue that needed dealing with.

The details were that, at the age of twelve, Louise had gone out for the day with a group of friends, travelling in a large van. At some point, a teenager in the party took advantage of the absence of everyone else, and raped Louise. As is so common in this kind of situation, Louise felt guilty and bad, and certainly didn't go home and tell her parents. We worked gently through the scenes, until the hurt subsided. Louise told me later, 'I knew it had worked, when I found that I could walk past large vans, without getting that pang of fear.'

For Louise the rest of her childhood was not happy; her self-esteem was gone and she was bullied at school. She married young, but the relationship was abusive, and she was separated again by 2001. That was when her troubles took a real turn for the worse. Her husband had been much involved with the ideas of 'Wicca':[1] he practised spells and spoke of spirit guides. This was a source of concern for Louise, as her background was as a practising Christian. It added to her already well-established sense of badness, making her feel that she might have become 'tainted with evil.'

Louise was already receiving help, and one day mentioned her evil-related anxieties to her community psychiatric nurse. What she was looking for was someone from whom to seek reassurance, not someone who would simply scoff at the silly notions of witches and magic. The advice she received was to telephone a support group called SAFE (Supporting Survivors of Sadistic/Satanic Abuse). It certainly didn't mean that Louise would be safe.

Over the course of the next two or three years, Louise was sucked in from making the occasional call, to being on the phone for a couple of hours every night. It all began innocuously enough, but when Louise mentioned distressing nightmares she was told that she couldn't have such dreams unless the imagined events had actually happened in the past. Naturally, she couldn't remember these events, but that, they explained, was because they had been repressed! The 'treatment' comprised hypnosis, although that label was never used; she was given deep relaxation instructions, and taken to the traditional 'safe place' of hypnotic inductions: a beach. So far, so good; no one could complain about a technique that produced a feeling of warm well-being. However, Louise then had to lie on the sand of her vividly imagined beach, and let the waves wash over her. With each wave a new memory would be uncovered. Of course, the 'memories' were elicited with appropriately leading questions and, no matter how bizarre, they were always accepted as veridical.

Bizarre the memories certainly were;[2] they would have sat very comfortably alongside the evidence of a Seventeenth Century witchcraft trial. She came to believe that half the congregation of her church was involved in satanic rituals, with abuse of babies and all manner of perverse goings-on. Naturally, Louise was abused, and particularly frightening for her was the fact that her own mother was a key figure in these practices. The Satanists were cunning and covered their tracks well. For divulging their misdeeds Louise was putting herself in danger, and for a while she actually moved to Scotland, to escape any possible retribution. When she moved further South again she was near enough to her old home to be able to notice inconsistencies between what she saw of the geography of the place, and the 'memories' that had become so vivid. Importantly, she witnessed her mother's caring behaviour towards a new grandson. Could these be the actions of a baby-sacrificing Satanist?

One day, a fellow 'survivor' mentioned the BFMS to Louise. The mention was not a kind one: they were an organisation of abusers, set up to protect others of their sort, she was told! Now, Louise has a stubborn streak; it has probably been the one thing that has kept her fighting on through all this. On this occasion it was certainly her salvation: as she put it, 'You have only to tell me to keep away from someone, and I'm in there straight away!'

So, in late 2003 Louise rang the BFMS. She spoke to Madeline, and received what felt like straightforward, unpressurising, common sense. This was the start of regular contact with Madeline, and also Pat, a member of the Society. Everything began to fall into place, and she could see how the 'memories' just couldn't be true. However, one problem remained. If the whole thing were a tissue of lies, how was it that she had believed it so absolutely? At the intellectual level she could appreciate that the stories were ridiculous, but her feelings still screamed that they were true. I had once helped another 'retractor' with similar difficulties, so Louise came for hypnosis.

I am always telling people that there is nothing magical about hypnosis, so how was it able to help? Well, Louise tells me that there were three helpful ingredients. First, the general reduction in fear and guilt (concerning the rape) gave her a better sense of security and self-belief. Second, she recognised the exact parallels between what I was doing under the overt 'hypnosis' label, and what had been done to her by SAFE; they really had hypnotised her and 'messed with my mind!' Obviously that could generate believable stories.

Perhaps most importantly, as Louise worked through the various images in her head she could feel the difference between the real and the false traumatic memories. She knew that there had never been a time when she didn't remember the rape, 'If I couldn't forget that, how come the satanic abuse memories could be hidden?'

Things really did seem to have fallen into place for Louise. It had been a terrible story, but the genuine trauma, perhaps the event that set her upon this disastrous path, had finally offered a means of eradicating the false. Nevertheless, it has to be recorded that simply rejecting the pseudo-memories has not made life entirely problem free for Louise. For a start, her dealings with the NHS were hampered for a long time, with key personnel reluctant to abandon the original wild and fantastic stories of abuse, and take in their place the simple explanation that they had been false memories. The long years of fear and unhappiness have left their mark too, but that stubborn streak is still keeping Louise fighting on; the last word must go to her. It was what she told me at the end of the telephone conversation in which she took me, step by step, through these sad events, 'You know, going through all this again hasn't upset me at all; it would have done once. I must have got things sorted!'

4. Lisa's story: a 'friend's' malign influence

Writing in 2009 from the USA, Lisa charts her journey towards realisation that her memories were not true and her reconciliation with her family and theirs with her.

It's hard to say just when I first began to realise that the memories of abuse were not real. I am clear, however, on when they began. It was during the five month period from November 1990 through March 1991.

For years before that time, I (as well as my mother and sister) suspected that there had been some sort of sexual molestation incident in my childhood that I was not remembering. This was based mainly on specific unexplained fears and what I'd called 'sensory memories' that I had experienced at least once a week, when in that state between sleep and wakefulness, from around the age of 8, and which lasted well into my adulthood. We brainstormed together over the years, thinking about everyone we could remember who had spent time at our house or had any other opportunity, but were never able to figure out who it might have been.

Telling that to Jane proved to be akin to handing over the vault combination to a bank robber.

Jane was a romantic partner I met over the telephone in November of 1990, only months after losing my job and falling into a financial tailspin and a depression that to this day is still the worst I've ever endured. At 26, I'd had to move back in with my parents. We'd always been a very close family, but I was besieged with my own feelings of failure and inadequacy, coupled with morbid depression (I've dealt with clinical depression since I was a teenager), and I saw it as the worst thing that could have happened. I was suicidal. I even had a plan. I was at the most vulnerable point I had ever been, or have been since.

Enter Jane, to whom I was introduced by a mutual friend who, at the time, I'd only just met. Our friend told me that some of the things I said and interests I spoke of reminded her of her friend, Jane, who, she'd said, was working out of state. She said she'd mentioned me to her and that Jane had enquired as to whether I would mind if she called me on the phone. At the time, I was nonchalant about it and didn't really put a lot of thought into the request.

'Sure,' I said, and she passed along my telephone number.

She did call, and we spoke by phone for five months, until the day she called to tell me she'd returned home. We then began an in-person relationship.

She was a controller and a manipulator, an expert and detailed liar, and fascinated with cults and brainwashing techniques. It was a dangerous combination. She'd read and studied cult indoctrination techniques for years and had learned from experience what worked and what did not when it came to convincing others to do her bidding. She was good. She was very good. She had also read and often quoted from *The courage to heal* and other self-help books with a similar message, as well as publications with a radical feminist agenda. She had a soothing voice and spoke intelligently and with an enthusiasm that often was contagious. She had a gift for making the object of her affections feel very special, as if there were no one else in the world she would rather be talking with.

She always called me, and I never knew her telephone number because, as she had explained to me, she'd been given a telephone expense account by her employer that allowed her to remain in touch with her family and friends while she was travelling. It made it easier, she said, to be so far from home, if she had 'phone friends'. Although Caller ID and *69 services were available in the United States by that time, my parents did not have them on the two lines into their house (one was for me) and on the one or two occasions I used *69 to try and find out where she was calling from, her number came up as Private. This was before cell phones were commonly used and she had said it would be easier if she just called me each time, because she had the expense account and because she would be calling from different hotel phones as she moved from place to place.

We spoke every evening, from the time I got off of work until late into the night, often falling asleep with the phone line still open. She would talk to me as I fell asleep, and I found it comforting.

At some point, I told her about my suspicions of sexual molestation, among the many other things we talked about. One evening, I was telling her about a short story I had read. It was about a young woman who confronted her father regarding his having sexually abused her as a child. I was affected by the story and had cried when I'd read it because I just couldn't imagine how difficult that would be. Jane commented about my reaction to the story.

'It's just so sad,' I'd said.

She said the reason I was affected emotionally by the story was because I identified with it.

'Don't you see?' she'd said, 'It was your father who molested you.'

26

I resisted the idea at first, but over the next several weeks, I began to experience flashes of memory: him standing over me as I lay in bed, terrified, him doing things that seemed to explain the 'sensory memories' I'd had for years.

Before long, in spite of how unlikely this devastating 'realisation' seemed, I believed — I 'knew' — that my father had done those unspeakable things. Jane said comforting things and assured me I was having these memories because I was finally ready to face them.

During the time that we spoke on the phone, she told me several intricately woven stories that I later found out were lies, including the one about her working out of state. She was actually across town the whole time, bedridden due to degenerative arthritis and other health problems. She didn't believe I would want to be with her if I knew of her disabilities, so she constructed a story about a car crash that left her injured, and went on to add to the story by telling me that the physical trauma of her injuries had caused her other health problems. Her story was just vague enough, and just detailed enough, that it sounded plausible.

There were times, though, when I knew, deep down, that she was lying about being out of state. I knew, but I chose to blindly ignore what I knew because, in my unhealthy mental state, I saw only two choices: close my eyes and 'jump' into a relationship with her, or continue with my suicide plan. I was completely unable to fathom that I had any *other* choices, including *not* becoming involved with her and *not* committing suicide. In an ironic way, she actually saved my life (in the process of tearing it apart).

We continued to talk, through the holidays, the New Year, Valentines Day, and then just before Easter, she called to say she was home. We met in person, I moved in with her, and I began to sever contact with my family and friends, one by one, at Jane's urging.

> They aren't able to love you the way you need to be loved.
> They're too dysfunctional. Being around them is detrimental
> to your healing process. They don't respect your reality. They're
> in denial. They'll never admit the things they've done to you.

I wrote awful letters to my parents and sister. I accused my father of sexually molesting me and I believed my mother knew about it and did nothing. I accused my family of not being emotionally supportive enough and of varying forms of verbal and emotional abuse. While these things weren't true, I wasn't lying. I absolutely believed them, with every bit of my being.

And I missed my family terribly.

Years went by. Two. Three. Four. I still suffered from depression in varying degrees, and every time I would allow myself to think about how much I missed my family, I would think that it was too late to go back. Too much damage had been done. At first, I believed it was the damage from the abuse they refused to admit to, and as time went by and my new memories started to fade, I began to see that the damage was the pain I knew I had caused them. The pain I was slowly beginning to suspect might not have been justified and which could never be taken back.

The new memories became cloudier and began to hold less power, while the 'sensory memories' I'd had all along never wavered in their intensity.

Finally, one day, after Jane and I had split up (but remained friends) and I'd moved into my own apartment a few blocks away, I was at her place, visiting, and I witnessed something shocking. Her new partner came into the living room, sobbing.

'I just remembered that my father raped me when I was a little girl,' she cried. I remembered that not long before that, Jane had taken me aside and whispered to me confidentially, in an excited voice, 'The other night, I hypnotised (her girlfriend).'

If I had to try to pin down a specific turning point in my realising that my memories weren't real, that day would be it.

In the spring of 1995, after having spoken with my mother a few times off and on, I called her and asked if we could meet as a family and talk. My family was extremely relieved and immediately arranged a meeting. A good friend of mine, of many years, who knew my family well and was a social worker by profession, agreed to go with me. We sat around my parents' dining room table and talked, cried, argued, cried some more, and managed to reconnect as a family. I apologised, to my entire family, and again, separately, to my dad. He said, 'It's all in the past now,' with tears in his eyes, and held me. Forgiven. No questions asked. That was when I learned not only what unconditional love was, but that I'd had it all along, all those years when I was being told that they weren't capable of it, and long before.

In the 14 years since then, we have forged an even closer bond, grown and changed as people, and I believe I became a much stronger person than I might have otherwise, had we never gone through it. I still don't know what, if anything, actually did happen to cause those fears and 'sensory memories', but they both finally went away when I was 39, after having dealt with some other fear-related issues in my life. I finally decided that it doesn't matter what happened, or whether anything did. If I did block out a difficult experience, that memory won't likely ever come back, and the best thing I can do for myself is let it go and work on achieving my goals and plans for the future. I am recently dealing, finally, with the last remnants of my guilt feelings about hurting my family and the confusion over how such a thing could happen.

And I'm learning that it did (and sadly, still does) happen to a vast number of people and that my situation was nowhere near as isolated as I previously thought it was.

Part II.

Psychology's dilemma

Introduction to Part II

Recovered memory is 'either the most fascinating psychological discovery of the 20th century or the centerpiece of the most embarrassing mistake modern psychiatry and psychotherapy have ever made.'

Richard Ofshe and Margaret Singer, University of California at Berkeley quoted in Loftus and Rosenwald [1993]

Do no harm?

The case histories featured in the previous Part of this book demonstrate how the origins of false memory are often rooted in a vulnerable person seeking help. This section aims to throw a little light on the environment in which (for the most part) well-meaning practitioners and social workers operate: an environment of fiercely-held beliefs in unproven theories of memory recovery where, even within the professions of psychiatry and psychology, the issue of memory is, as Professor McNally is quoted at the start of this book, 'the flashpoint of one of the most bitter controversies ever to afflict the fields of psychology and psychiatry.'

'Roses and reminiscences'

It was like an episode in science fiction. I can see it in my mind's eye now, though it was nearly 40 years ago: a dense, high wall of pink roses reaching up like a giant cobra about to strike, and advancing silently, menacingly, across the lawn towards us. Then it collapsed in a waist-deep tangle of sweet-scented confusion. I discovered that the rope linking it to the shed supporting it had snapped.

As I thought back to that summer afternoon I said to your mum: do you remember when those roses collapsed? And she replied: 'You weren't there. You hadn't got home from work when that happened. I just told you about it.'

I can see the wall of roses looming well above head high. I can see it teeter, then topple and collapse.

But I wasn't there.

(A father's letter to his daughter — not sent)

(BFMS Forum 2009)

5. A psychologist's view: 'Repression is a theory, not a fact'

Professor Larry Weiskrantz FRS, Emeritus Professor of Psychology, University of Oxford (First published in Fractured families, *[Brand, 2007])*

Everyone is aware of the frustration of inaccessible memories, when we cannot recall something that we wish to do, like finding a name, or recalling an event from childhood that must have occurred, or when we fail to recognise a person who appears totally unfamiliar until he proceeds to recount to us when and where we met. Much less familiar is the phenomenon of remembering something to which we have no right — because it is an event that never occurred.

There is now abundant laboratory evidence for the creation of such false memories [Brainerd and Reyna, 2005]. They are relatively easy phenomena to generate if a powerful, and repetitive suggestion is made by an authoritative and persuasive mentor, and especially if it is within the context of a compelling wider framework. Clearly false memories can play a dangerous role in witness testimony and other claims for the recall of non-existent or seriously distorted events. The most serious examples, perhaps, are accusations of severe sexual abuse that never occurred, although fervently believed by the accuser. A person who is the target of such an accusation can have his or her life deeply and irrevocably damaged. It is not only fractured families who emerge, but tragically fractured and shattered individuals. And subsequently, if the truth finally emerges, damage can rebound upon the accuser.

The most common context within which these emerge is in forms of therapy based on the tenet that many problems of everyday life, both physical but especially psychological, have developed because of childhood abuse, a view propounded in books such as *The courage to heal* [Bass and Davis, 1988] and other treatises. If the client in such a therapeutic regime cannot remember any such abuse, the claim is that it must have been deeply repressed and made inaccessible, but with appropriate therapy the memory can be 'recovered'. And, indeed, clients can come honestly to be persuaded that the recovered memory must be true even if it is not.

There is no solid experimental evidence, as such, for the core tenet of this approach, the repression of traumatic memories. Of course, it is not an easy matter to investigate in the laboratory, and the matter has been controversial for over 100 years. But two Harvard psychiatrists, Drs Harrison Pope and James Hudson [1995], carried out a determined and thorough search some 10 years ago of the published literature for reliable, acceptable evidence of the repression of memories of sexual abuse, and failed to find a single example or study that stood up to rigorous test. (See articles about their research and implications in *The London Times*, 16 March and 11 April, 1995; see, also, a review by another Harvard psychologist, Richard J. McNally [2004]). Repression is a theory, not a fact. Theory aside, there is ample evidence that, on the contrary, those who have suffered traumatic stress have the opposite problem — it is not that they cannot remember but they that they have trouble in forgetting the trauma.

By now there is an accumulation of large numbers of examples of accusations of childhood sexual abuse having been made for which evidence subsequently demonstrated that they could not have happened. It is rare for anyone who has been the object of such a false accusation easily to recover from such an experience, especially if made by a loved one, even if the charge is demonstrated to be false. These are compound fractures that may never heal. Childhood abuse is, of course, a dire problem not to be underestimated. But adult abuse by fervent accusers often of a crusading vigilante nature, based on events that never occurred, is a life shattering experience.

6. Creating nightmares: a short history of belief in ritual abuse

Katharine J Mair, Consultant Clinical Psychologist (retired)

What is ritual abuse?

The Ritual Abuse Information Network and Support group (RAINS) has defined ritual abuse as 'sexual abuse occurring in the context of symbols or activities ... used repeatedly to frighten children.' Another definition is of abuse 'that occurs in ceremonial or circumscribed manner for the purpose of creating or manipulating already created alter mental states' [Noblitt and Noblitt, 2008]. Neither of these definitions conveys the full horror of ritual abuse, which includes unspeakably disgusting, cruel and criminal acts. These are said to be inflicted on children, often from infancy, by an organised group of people. Experiences reported by alleged survivors of this abuse include repeated rape, cannibalism, torture, being caged, being forced to participate in murders, animal mutilations and to ingest blood and other bodily fluids [Rutz et al., 2008].

How do we know about this? No traces of these crimes have ever been found, and none of the perpetrators has ever been brought to justice. We know of these crimes only through the testimony of the alleged victims. Their testimony is nearly always produced after they have been in therapy, and this therapy will usually have followed a diagnosis of dissociative identity disorder (DID), a new name for what used to be called multiple personality disorder (MPD). People suffering from this disorder will spontaneously adopt different personalities, called alters, and speak as though they were completely different people. In therapy the client will talk, through the alters, to a therapist who understands this condition: 'This is long term psychotherapy; it takes years, probably a minimum of five years ... It often takes two or more years to establish enough trust for the client to be able to disclose any important information' [Miller, 2008].

It is clear that many people all over the world do believe they have suffered unimaginable horrors. Their therapists are convinced that powerful cults continue to terrorise both children and adults, and that only a few of their victims have the courage to seek help. For them this is an under-reported problem. Yet for others it is simply unbelievable that abuse on such a scale should be going on.

How did this come about?

Belief in ritual abuse can be traced to two very influential, best-selling books. Both of them tell the story of someone who discovered, while in therapy, that they had been abused from early childhood. The first was *Sybil* [Schreiber, 1973]. This was written by a journalist, and described the eleven year long psychoanalysis of Sybil Dorset undertaken by Dr Cornelia Wilbur. During this therapy Sybil suddenly started assuming different personalities, switching between them in the apparently involuntary way that indicated multiple personality disorder (MPD). At this time MPD was still thought to be a very rare condition which had been linked in the past to possession by spirits or supernatural powers, and more recently to a variety of psychological and neurological disorders. However Dr Wilbur, who had welcomed the opportunity of undertaking the first ever psychoanalysis of a multiple personality, assumed from the start that Sybil's 'dissociation' resulted, not from any current problems she might have had, but from something in her past. She thought it must have started during childhood, possibly to distance Sybil from some trauma, and that to discover what this trauma was, she would have to ask the alternative personalities rather than the more reserved and rational host personality. These alters were encouraged to emerge, sometimes through hypnosis. Over time nineteen of them appeared — each was named and treated as a reliable informant. As expected, they spoke of childhood trauma, weird maltreatment by Sybil's mother, of which Sybil herself had been unaware.

The supposition that dissociation in an adult was a sign of severe childhood trauma established a model for treating MPD which has been followed to this day. Although full scale dissociation has always been seen in adults rather than children, therapists from now on believed that it started, long before it could be observed, in early childhood. From Dr Wilbur onwards any current explanations for dissociation were discounted, and fostering instead the belief in childhood trauma, therapists encouraged the emergence of alters. Since these alters were often children, therapy would often involve an adult therapist talking to someone as if they were a child. The supposition was that alters had been adopted by abused children to protect them from full awareness of what was happening to them, and, most importantly, it was the alters rather than the host that held the memories of this trauma. From now on dissociation was no longer seen as an aberration to be controlled, but as a useful diagnostic indicator of childhood abuse.

Dr Wilbur never attempted to corroborate her conjectures, and could get no peer reviewed psychiatric journal to publish her account of Sybil's treatment. However, her friend's second-hand, journalistic account became a best-selling book which was later made into a film. This was followed by a rapid increase in the diagnosis of MPD in the United States, and by 1980 it received official recognition by being included for the first time in the *Diagnostic and statistical manual of mental disorders* of the American Psychiatric Association [1980].

Sybil, even in her most dissociated state, never reported any ritual abuse. Was this because her therapist had never heard of it? No accounts of ritual abuse had appeared until 1980, when another best-selling book, *Michelle Remembers* [Smith and Pazder, 1980], gave us the first ritual abuse 'survivor' story, co-written with the psychiatrist who had uncovered the abuse. It detailed Michelle's sexual abuse and torture by a group of Satanists, including her parents. She had witnessed the ritual murders of babies and adults and had been made to eat the ashes of one of the victims; she had also been caged and tormented with spiders and snakes. Her torture had culminated in a visit from Satan, but she was saved by the intervention of the Virgin Mary and Jesus. Like Sybil, Michelle was found to have MPD. She revealed details of her abuse during therapy with Dr Pazder, who had previously worked in West Africa studying black magic rituals. These revelations were strenuously denied by members of Michelle's family, and no corroborating evidence was ever found. However, the book was a great success, achieving massive sales and publicity. Pazder then married Michelle, and together they profited from their new-found celebrity, appearing frequently on television and radio. Television talk shows in the States during the 80s started featuring topics such as 'Satanic breeders: Babies for sacrifice,' and 'Investigating multiple personalities: Did the Devil make them do it?' The Pazders frequently spoke at conferences, as experts on satanic cult ritual abuse [Victor, 1993].

In the US and Canada there was a growing interest both in ritual abuse and in MPD during the 1980s. Both were being reported with unprecedented frequency, and they increasingly went together. MPD had previously been dismissed by many psychiatrists and psychologists as iatrogenic, i.e. generated by therapists in suggestible, fantasy-prone clients [Merskey, 1992]. However, by the end of the decade it was suggested that 1% of the population might have MPD [Ross, 1991]. This was bad news, since by then many therapists believed that MPD was always a sign of severe child abuse. What made the news even worse was their belief that the truth about what had happened during childhood would be found, not by taking a careful history from their adult clients, nor by checking their background details, but by inviting the alters to tell them what they knew. Thus clients would inform therapists while they were in an altered state of consciousness, often speaking with the voice of a child, sometimes after deliberately induced hypnosis. Therapists duly found their suspicions confirmed, so that gruesome tales of organised rape, torture and murder, 'remembered' by their clients and recounted to their therapists, were leading to widespread anxiety about what might be happening to today's children. Preschool day care centres were singled out for suspicion, and many very young children were intensively questioned or examined for 'signs of abuse.' Between 1984 and 1989 these investigations in the US led to the arrest of 100 men and women, of whom 50 were tried and convicted. All verdicts were later overturned, when the lack of any corroborating evidence was revealed [Victor, 1993].

Looking out for ritual abuse in the UK

Perhaps it was inevitable that what has been described as a 'moral panic' in North America should later spread to the UK and across the world. In 1989 Pamela Klein, a 'ritual abuse counsellor,' and Jerry Simandl, a youth officer with the Chicago police department, visited Britain and gave a series of presentations to professionals working with adults and children. I attended one of these myself and experienced its powerful effect. Klein and Simandl spoke with authority about the practice of Satanism, the organisation of the cults, and the methods used to intimidate their victims, confusing them so that their testimony would not be believed. At this meeting there was little time for reflection or questions. It was not until much later that I wondered how they were able to be so specific about the practices of the Satanists, since no cult members had ever been identified. Most of us had never heard of ritual abuse before, and probably most people left in a state of shock, thinking, as I did, 'Oh dear! I'll have to look out for this now.' In my work as a clinical psychologist I did look out for it, and at one time I thought I had found it, until I realised that exposure to horror videos provided a far more likely explanation for this person's strange ideas.

Other professionals who had been at this presentation also looked out for ritual abuse and were more easily convinced. Included amongst them were child protection social workers from Rochdale, who were later responsible for removing seventeen children from their parents. This action had been sparked off by bizarre stories of black magic and baby killing from a six year old boy. The children's responses to intensive questioning persuaded the social workers that they were all victims of an abusive satanic cult. A judicial inquiry later found that there was no evidence for this, the social workers and local police were severely criticised, and the children were eventually returned to their parents. Similar actions from social workers who had been alarmed by the testimony of ritual abuse 'experts,' led to children being removed from their parents in Orkney and in Nottingham. In each case no evidence of any ritual abuse was found, and the children were returned home [Waterhouse, 1990b,a].

In 1991 the Government, concerned about all these happenings, commissioned Jean La Fontaine, an anthropologist, to carry out an investigation into the existence of ritual abuse cults in the UK. She found no evidence of the type of organised abuse that was being reported by various therapists, carers and alleged victims, and considered that many of the 'disclosures' by young children were largely suggested by the adults interviewing them [La Fontaine, 1994].

Meanwhile, now that ritual abuse was in the public consciousness, professionals working with adults were also seeking and finding it. In the clinical psychology department where I worked we had all by now heard of ritual abuse, but most of us saw no evidence of its effects in our clients. However, just a few of my colleagues did see such evidence, and they saw it repeatedly. Some of them were now quite upset at repeatedly having to listen to accounts of such gruesome abuse. When I raised this anomaly with a colleague, who at this time had several clients reporting ritual abuse, she explained that information about ritual abuse was 'often hesitatingly given, testing out the therapist with snippets of details.' Clearly it took a therapist who was able to join the dots. It also helped that they had no qualms about diagnosing MPD or, as it now came to be known, dissociative identity disorder (DID). Ritual abuse was only disclosed to the few psychologists in our department who did diagnose this condition. Before they started therapy, none of their clients had apparently been aware that they had been ritually abused as children.

RAINS conference 2001

After I retired I remained curious about how some therapists were able to maintain their beliefs about ritual abuse. The La Fontaine report had now been published, as had studies by psychologists throwing doubt on the reliability of any 'memories' that were only recovered during therapy. There had been widespread concern about children wrongly taken into care, and parents who had been unjustly accused of horrible crimes. In 1994 the British False Memory Society had been established to support these parents, and to focus the concerns of many professionals working in this area.

It was therefore with interest that in 2001 I attended a conference organised jointly by RAINS (Ritual Abuse Information Network and Support) and The Clinic for Dissociative Studies. Both these organisations supported therapists who diagnosed ritual abuse, and 'survivors' who reported it. At this conference I found myself surrounded by about 180 therapists and survivors, none of whom appeared to share my scepticism, though they were aware of a 'backlash.' This had made the work of those who continued to believe in ritual abuse more difficult. Psychotherapist Valerie Sinason was spurred into developing her own clinic because the Tavistock Clinic, where she previously held the post of child psychotherapist, declined to support further work with ritual abuse survivors. Several speakers at the conference referred to the sacrifices that were made by those who persisted in their efforts to uncover cases of ritual abuse or treat the survivors. One thing that all the adverse publicity did not seem to have done was to change the minds of any of those who were already committed to a belief in ritual abuse.

Valerie Sinason acknowledged that believers in ritual abuse had a problem when trying to convince others of their beliefs: their knowledge of ritual abuse came solely from the testimony of alleged survivors. None had been able to provide independent, incontrovertible evidence of what had occurred. 'There is a hole in the middle,' she admitted. After more than a decade of searching, no relics of the reported gruesome ceremonies had been found: no bones, no bloodstains, and no bodies. There had been some successful prosecutions for child sexual abuse accompanied by strange and frightening rituals, but these did not in any way match the horrors reported by most ritual abuse survivors. Their stories always included killings, usually several of them, but there had been no prosecutions for ritual murder. She called for more research to convince others of the reality of ritual abuse, but the only method she was able to suggest was working with the survivors to provide more information on their experiences and their circumstances. This would hardly fill the hole.

Therapists at this conference had been impressed by the way their different clients told similar stories featuring cages, cannibalism, the use of bodily fluids and murder. Their clients also told of being coerced into carrying out unspeakable practices themselves so that they would be incriminated and unable to free themselves from the cult. This enabled the therapists to speak with conviction about a wide variety of cult practices and to know what to look for with new clients. A survivor told me how grateful she was that, after years of treatment with one therapist, she had gone to another one who immediately recognised the physical signs and other pointers to ritual abuse, thus enabling her to recall the details during eight more years of therapy. A history of ritual abuse was said to be hard to detect since most survivors usually have no conscious memories of it before going into therapy. Even when they do remember, they are said to be reluctant to tell their stories, because they are afraid both of the continuing power of the cult, and of being disbelieved by the people they turn to.

What had given the people at this conference their invincible belief in ritual abuse? In most cases it was their experience of being told 'this happened to me,' usually by a very disturbed and distressed individual. 'No one would put themselves through that torment if it wasn't true.' 'When you have eye contact with somebody . . . you know.' 'As soon as she started talking I knew she was a survivor.' 'When you sit in front of someone who is a genuine DID case, you cannot disbelieve.' Several people spoke of the increased severity of the revelations as their receptiveness increased. 'Everything I touched seemed to escalate.' 'The abuse stories got unbelievably worse' — but still she believed! Therapists themselves were often traumatised by what the clients were telling them, and this powerful experience may have strengthened a bond in which any questioning of testimony was quite unthinkable.

Norma Howes, a social worker and therapist for both adults and children, told the conference that she was working with someone who did not know whether her memories were real or dreams: 'Therapeutically it doesn't matter. If your dreams require metaphor of such horror, then something awful must have happened to you.' She did add that you cannot use such information in the courts, because 'what is compelling in therapy is not in the courts.'

I had the impression that at least half of the clients seen by these therapists had DID. This was seen by itself as an indicator of severe abuse from an early age. There was much talk of how to deal with the various alters. They held important memories of the abuse, but they also served different functions, and not all of them were helpful. Some of them might be loyal to the cult which had abused them, or to their parents. Some might make allegations that were patently ridiculous (such as being abused by aliens), and some might try to disrupt the therapy. This was attributed to 'programming' by the cult. Children were deliberately confused, so that their testimony would not be believed. Several speakers mentioned 'mind control' and the use of torture and deprivation to enslave the child and make him or her terrified of telling anybody.

Clients do not simply describe abuse and torture; they also appear to re-experience it during the therapy sessions. They may scream and whimper and try to hide. They can even show bodily changes such as the spontaneous appearance of burns and wounds. Similar phenomena have been produced experimentally, using hypnosis, but the mechanism is hard to explain and the effect is uncanny. Several therapists at the conference mentioned physical manifestations in their clients, either observed during therapy or occurring outside it. They explained these as 'body memories:' the body is remembering and re-experiencing what happened to it previously. Valerie Sinason even suggested that some unexplained physical problems occurring at the present time could be seen as evidence that earlier abuse had occurred. For example, gynaecological pain could indicate earlier sexual assault, and food allergies could be a reaction to earlier enforced cannibalism. She also claimed that full-blown DID was 'proof' of earlier torture.

The therapists who believe in ritual abuse seem to have an answer for many things that the rest of us find puzzling. Why do people who claim to be survivors of long-term ritual abuse usually have no memory of this before they go into therapy? Until recently the disputed mechanism of repression was invoked. However recent research on the brain functioning of people who had been subjected to known trauma, such as fires or other severe accidents, has suggested that memories of trauma are processed rather differently from other memories, bypassing that area of the brain, the hippocampus, that is involved in laying down long term memories. Some victims of known trauma appear to have a slightly shrunken hippocampus. Two speakers told the conference that this research could be useful in providing some explanation for memory difficulties in ritually abused clients. No information seemed to be available on the states of their hippocampi, however, so it was hard to see how this research on people who had suffered a completely different type of sudden trauma could be applied. Also it seems rather paradoxical to suggest that the survivors who provide the therapists with all their detailed knowledge of ritual abuse are suffering from damage to the part of the brain that is involved in long-term memory.

The chair of RAINS, psychiatrist Dr Joan Coleman, said that RAINS accepted the reality of false memories, but thought they were less likely to be induced by therapy than by the perpetrators of ritual abuse. She pointed out that these people induced false memories deliberately, using many methods, including drugs and hypnosis. These false memories were of happenings, such as alien abduction, that are so fantastic that they will discredit the testimony of the victims. Until the last session of the conference I heard no warnings to therapists that they might unwittingly induce false memories. At this final session we were addressed by a panel of speakers including Norma Howes. She said that hypnosis must not be used to elicit memories, though it could be used in other ways to help clients. She did not elaborate on this and her message was somewhat obscured by another panel member, a survivor, who said that she totally disagreed. 'I would never have recovered my memories without hypnosis.' This remark was not challenged.

I heard no dissent at this conference. Therapists and survivors shared a powerful belief system that seemed bizarre to outsiders, but which was proof against all attacks and even seemed strengthened by the criticism it provoked. When I tentatively suggested that some aspects of survivor accounts seemed incredible, I was quickly told that some stories may be muddled because of the drugs and programming that survivors have received while in the cult, but that they are always essentially true: 'the abuse is real.' When I queried how survivors had been able to complete their education, sometimes to university level, and to function so well after a childhood of unremitting suffering, I was reminded of the wonderfully protective effect of dissociation.

I did not raise the question of the lack of physical evidence of murders, tortures and large gatherings, because I had already heard the answer: cult members had infiltrated many influential professions, and were found in the police, the legal system, parliament and the National Health Service. Thus, prosecution could be avoided and evidence destroyed, for example, by doctors disposing of bodies in hospital incinerators.

Believers in ritual abuse have answers for everything, and can speak with impressive conviction. Sceptics, by their very nature, are doubters, who ask questions rather than give answers. I found that I could not change the views of the believers, but neither could I dismiss these people as simple-minded or crazy. The therapists I met seemed to be intelligent, caring and conscientious people, genuinely wanting to relieve the suffering of their clients, while acknowledging that therapy was inevitably disturbing and that clients had to get worse before they could get better. Although no independent studies had demonstrated any benefits from this therapy, it seemed to be here to stay. Therapists and clients believed in it, and the more they engaged in it, the more their beliefs were reinforced.

Ritual abuse today

Nine years after that conference I wondered whether anything had changed. Criticism of the whole concept of ritual abuse has certainly continued, and a recent American book promoting awareness of ritual abuse, *Ritual abuse in the twenty-first century*, gives considerable space to deploring the campaigns of some sceptics. Two DID therapists have now been successfully sued by their clients for implanting false memories, and 'backlash interests' have been successful in the courts and the media in debates about ritual abuse.

> Organisations ... have extended their influence over the direction in which criminal and civil investigations are conducted and resolved [Noblitt and Noblitt, 2008].

Elsewhere the literature on false memory is criticised for being both political and polemical and even sometimes 'hysterical,' but its effectiveness is reluctantly acknowledged:

> Whereas in the past the general reliability of human memory — even to a large extent 'recovered' memory — was never seriously questioned, the FMS (false memory syndrome) publicity campaign has had the odd effect of casting doubt on whether memory itself can be trusted [Raschke, 2008].

In this country both the Royal College of Psychiatrists and the British Psychological Society have issued guidelines for their members, warning them of the unreliability of memory, and the difficulties faced by therapists when dealing with past events. The British Psychological Society warns that 'it is not really possible to establish whether a memory represents factual events without external corroboration' and also advises that:

> psychologists should avoid being drawn into a search for memories of abuse . . . Psychologists should avoid engaging in activities and techniques which are intended to reveal indications of past sexual abuse of which the client has no memory [British Psychological Society, 2000].

Many clients would have been spared the distress of believing that they had been ritually abused if only their therapists had followed this advice. My impression is that clinical psychologists working in the NHS are now more aware of the dangers of prompting false memories, and are far less likely to diagnose DID or to discover ritual abuse. Sadly, however, there is now a growing band of independent, unregulated therapists who work privately and are unlikely ever to see any guidelines. It seemed to me that at the 2001 RAINS conference, nearly all the therapists were in private practice, often with no recognised training or supervision.

In 2009 RAINS, in conjunction with an organisation called Trauma and Abuse Group (TAG), held a further conference. I attended this and discovered that little had changed in the previous eight years. This time there were approximately 200 delegates; most of them were therapists or counsellors working for small, independent organisations. Many said that they were new to this kind of work, and spoke of their amazement at encountering dissociated personalities and of their horror at hearing their disclosures. I also met people who identified themselves as survivors of ritual abuse. Some had been in therapy for many years, but some had moved on and were now themselves offering therapy to other survivors. Several had written books about their experiences. Once again there was an air of excitement about the demanding work of uncovering horrors. 'We are all pioneers,' declared one of the speakers, a Canadian psychologist, 'This is cutting edge therapy, not the Mickey Mouse stuff you hear about in graduate school.'

All the speakers at this conference were in private practice and spoke authoritatively about the continuing reality of ritual abuse. The continuing lack of any external evidence for this did not seem to discourage them. Reference was briefly made to set-backs, especially in the United States, from sceptics who had successfully sued therapists and stopped some people from coming forward. However, delegates were simply told to avoid getting caught up in 'the false memory controversy,' and were reassured that the tide was now turning. I reluctantly felt that this could well be true. I was impressed, as I had been in 2001, by the dedication and uncritical enthusiasm of both delegates and speakers, and by the support that they provided for each other in exploring their nightmarish worlds. Awareness of external criticism had simply driven these believers into each others' arms and away from all restraining influences.

The detection of ritual abuse and the treatment of its 'survivors' now seems to be mainly restricted to the unregulated fringes of therapeutic activity. This can make it even more dangerous. Seemingly magical therapies are flourishing all around us. They often engender a placebo effect of well-being, and many people are happy to try remedies without questioning where they come from or how they are supposed to work. One can only hope these people will be wary of any self-styled counsellor or healer who claims to understand the strange phenomenon of dissociation. If anything in their behaviour leads their therapist into diagnosing DID, they in turn will be led into a complete rewriting of their personal history. Major life changes may follow, as ties with family and friends are severed. Those who previously supported them may now be seen, at best, as unhelpful disbelievers, at worst, as members of a murderous cult. With prolonged therapy (and it usually is prolonged) the break can be very far reaching. A 'Christian counsellor' reports:

> What Laura and I only discovered years later, from her other personalities, was that neighbours were involved in the ritual group, as were teachers at her school, and the family doctor, so that those whom Laura thought as a child might offer her safety were perpetrators too [Cook, 2008].

Poor Laura! She now has only her therapist for support.

7. *Guidelines on memory and the law*: *recommendations from the scientific study of human memory*

Question marks over reliability of memory

In July 2008 the British Psychological Society launched a set of guidelines which it stated were to provide people who work in the law with the latest scientific evidence to consider issues relating to memory.

The 50-page document, lucidly argued and including nearly 20 pages of references closely linked to the main text, raises general issues of concern as to the reliability of individual memory. And to those whose principal concern is the reliability of allegations of historical abuse, it may seem especially vital that its arguments are scrutinised and, indeed, heeded by the legal profession and the courts.

A press release issued at the time by the Society has the headline: **Can the law trust your memory?** It says in part: 'Witnesses' memories are vital to the law and justice but memory is much more fallible than we realise.'

The report is the culmination of a working party set up by the Research Board of the British Psychological Society to study the latest evidence on human memory and how that evidence could be of use to the legal professions.

The report has some sobering key points on the reliability of people's memories in court cases. Key points of *Guidelines on memory and the law* include:

- The content of memories arises from an individual's comprehension of an experience, both conscious and non-conscious. This content can be further modified and changed by subsequent recall

- Any account of a memory will feature forgotten details and gaps

- People can remember events that they have not in reality experienced.

Professor Martin Conway of Leeds University, Chair of the Working Party, said,

In many legal cases, memory may feature as the main, or the only source of evidence, and is nearly always critical to the course and outcome of the case or litigation. It is therefore vital that those involved in legal work are well informed of developments in the scientific study of memory — how memories are created, their content, and how they are remembered, for example.

There is a tendency for people involved in the criminal justice system to influence witnesses' memories of events, intentional or unintentionally. This might be by asking leading questions or by reinforcing memories while recapping what a witness has said.

We have developed these guidelines to provide an accessible and scientifically accurate basis from which they can consider relevant legal issues relating to memory.

The document was revised and reissued in April 2010; it lists the following key points:

i. *Memories are records of people's experiences of events and are not a record of the events themselves.* In this respect, they are unlike other recording media such as videos or audio recordings, to which they should not be compared.

ii. *Memory is not only of experienced events but it is also of the knowledge of a person's life, i.e. schools, occupations, holidays, friends, homes, achievements, failures, etc.* As a general rule memory is more likely to be accurate when it is of the knowledge of a person's life than when it is of specific experienced events.

iii. *Remembering is a constructive process.* Memories are mental constructions that bring together different types of knowledge in an act of remembering. As a consequence, memory is prone to error and is easily influenced by the recall environment, including police interviews and cross-examination in court.

iv. *Memories for experienced events are always incomplete.* Memories are time-compressed fragmentary records of experience. Any account of a memory will feature forgotten details and gaps, and this must not be taken as any sort of indicator of accuracy. Accounts of memories that do not feature forgetting and gaps are highly unusual.

v. *Memories typically contain only a few highly specific details.* Detailed recollection of the specific time and date of experiences is normally poor, as is highly specific information such as the precise recall of spoken conversations. As a general rule, a high degree of very specific detail in a long-term memory is unusual.

vi. *Recall of a single or several highly specific details does not guarantee that a memory is accurate or even that it actually occurred.* In general, the only way to establish the truth of a memory is with independent corroborating evidence.

vii. *The content of memories arises from an individual's comprehension of an experience, both conscious and non-conscious.* This content can be further modified and changed by subsequent recall.

viii. *People can remember events that they have not in reality experienced.* This does not necessarily entail deliberate deception. For example, an event that was imagined, was a blend of a number of different events, or that makes personal sense for some other reason, can come to be genuinely experienced as a memory, (*these are often referred to as 'confabulations'*).

ix. *Memories for traumatic experiences, childhood events, interview and identification practices, memory in younger children and older adults and other vulnerable groups all have special features.* These are features that are unlikely to be commonly known by a non-expert, but about which an appropriate memory expert will be able to advise a court.

x. *A memory expert is a person who is recognised by the memory research community to possess knowledge relevant to the particular case.* It is recommended that, in addition to current requirements, those acting as memory expert witnesses be required to submit their full *curriculum vitae* to the court as evidence of their expertise.

8. The regulation of psychotherapy

The final chapter in the long debate over the regulation of psychotherapy?

Subject to government acceptance of the Health Professions Council (HPC) recommendations published on 10 December 2009 [Health Professions Council, 2009c], regulation of the counselling and psychotherapy industry could be introduced as early as 2011.[1] This will herald the end of a 30-year-long and often acrimonious debate between those, on the one hand, who believe that self-regulation is sufficient and that psychotherapists and counsellors should be free from impediment to develop their relationships with clients, appropriate to their (clients') needs, and, on the other, those who believe that the processes practised by therapists and counsellors, particularly those without proper or, indeed, any training, are capable of inflicting such harm on clients that statutory regulation is essential.

The HPC's Psychotherapists and Counsellors Professional Liaison Group (PLG) received over 1,000 responses during the consultation period. The HPC's position, following the consultation period, was given in the press statement made by the Council's Chief Executive, Marc Seale:

> Based on the work undertaken to date, the HPC is confident that its system can accommodate the regulatory needs of psychotherapists and counsellors. Statutory regulation would seek to enhance public protection by protecting commonly recognised professional titles and providing a fair and appropriate complaints system. It would also seek to protect the professionals by removing incompetent and unethical practitioners from practising and potentially harming the public, and thus reducing damage to the industry's reputation.

However, a worrying omission is the absence of any reference to hypnotherapists. Madeline Greenhalgh asks:

> If hypnotherapists do not fall under the psychotherapy umbrella will they be able to practise outside of any planned Government

> legislation, thus leaving the public in the unimproved position of protecting themselves from harm? [Greenhalgh, 2009]

Following a request by the BFMS for clarification, the HPC later defined their position on hypnotherapy, as follows,

> The work that we have undertaken has focused on the regulation of psychotherapists and counsellors and does not include hypnotherapists. We recognise that there is a potential overlap between the two. However, the work that has been undertaken only related to proposals that HPC is making for regulating psychotherapists and counsellors. When consulting on our proposals, we asked respondents to identify the impact that the proposals might have on the regulation of other psychological therapists. Whilst the term, 'other psychological therapists' is not defined within the White Paper, we have taken it to include hypnotherapists. As a result, whilst the work undertaken so far has focused on psychotherapists and counsellors, the government has identified that other psychological therapies are also a priority for statutory regulation in the future.

Key points from the report and FAQs

The HPC would be able to take legal action to prevent those who are not registered with the HPC or fail to fulfil its minimum standards from practising under the titles of psychotherapist or counsellor.

The HPC is at pains to stress that the standards it sets are 'broad enabling standards which do not affect the therapeutic relationship' (FAQ 5) and 'do not act as an unfair barrier to innovation or diversity' (FAQ 3). However it also emphasises that statutory regulation provides 'a way in which complaints can be dealt with fairly and appropriately' so that

> the very small minority of practitioners who do not practice [sic] safely and effectively can be removed from the Register and prevented from continuing to practise and continuing to cause harm.

> At the moment, a psychotherapist or counsellor who is removed from the membership of their professional body, for example, can simply continue in practice without any legal means for preventing continuing harm to members of the public (FAQ 2).

Thus they will be brought into line with the complaints system and disciplinary procedures that apply to the 14 health professions already regulated by the HPC.[2]

An idea of how these disciplinary proposals will affect counsellors and psychotherapists can be gained from the Calendar of Events on the HPC's website, under 'Fitness to Practise Hearings.'

The Register will be structured to differentiate between the titles 'psychotherapist' and 'counsellor,' both of which will become protected titles (FAQ 6). The important issue, however, lies in the decision to make these titles 'non-modality specific.' Briefly this would prevent practitioners from adding adjectives before the protected title in order to avoid registration, 'For example, someone using the title 'psychodynamic' in front of psychotherapist would need to be registered' [Health Professions Council, 2009d, p. 17].

Registers of existing members of voluntary organisations (numbering over 30) will be transferred to the HPC. There are many conditions that apply to this procedure [2009d, pp. 27–31]. There will be a 'grandparenting' period — i.e. a period of 'grace' — two years is proposed — during which

> individuals who have not been members of one of the voluntary registers, and who do not hold an approved qualification ... but who have been in practice before the opening date of the HPC Register, can apply for registration [2009d, p. 32].

Minimum standards of proficiency will be introduced, as follows:

a) For counsellors, level 5 on the National Qualifications Framework/level 5 on the Framework for Higher Education Qualifications/level 8/9 on the Scottish Credit and Qualifications Framework.

b) For psychotherapists, level 7 on the National Qualifications Framework/level 7 on the Framework for Higher Education Qualifications/ level 11 on the Scottish Credit and Qualifications Framework. [2009d, p. 45].

Registrants must renew their registration every two years and must undertake continuing professional development. Samples of those renewing their registration will be audited to ensure they meet the standards (FAQ 11).

9. A parent's view: the Kafkaesque world of 'recovered memories'

It is difficult, if not impossible, for anyone who has not 'been there' to imagine themselves into the Kafkaesque world of so-called 'recovered memory' therapy, and all its dreadful consequences for the innocent victims[1].

This is a world where an adult, while undergoing psychotherapy, comes to 'remember' in vivid and colourful detail being emotionally, physically or sexually abused in early childhood (usually by a father or mother, or both, or siblings, grandparents, uncles, aunts, family friends, teachers, carers or voluntary workers).

This is a world where innocent adults are suddenly confronted with allegations against which they have no emotional or informed defence, for they invariably have no foreknowledge of how and why they came to be made. All that they know is that they are not true. But protestations of innocence do not convince the accuser.

It is a world where, even if (as in a number of cases) it is proven beyond all doubt that the 'memories' could not have happened, the accuser remains unconvinced (or, understandably, is unable to face up to the truth, although the fault is not theirs but the psychotherapist's) and many on the 'outside' will suspect that 'there is no smoke without fire.'

Yet for some of those accused, the nightmare does not end when the accuser has departed, often for good, leaving behind shattered adults and broken families. In a significant minority of cases, the allegations are reported to the police and social services by the 'believer.' While the accuser is guaranteed anonymity, the identity of the alleged perpetrator is divulged to the media.

The consequences can be equally hard to imagine. As the 'Brandon' Report said:

> The effects of such distorted truth should not be overlooked. The damage done to families if the accusations are untrue is immense. Moreover, it is not only families that are damaged by mistakes in this area. Patients who are mistakenly diagnosed as having been abused frequently end as mental health casualties. Where apparent improvement is based upon a false belief, there seems

> a serious possibility of further mental distress [Brandon et al.,
> 1998, p. 304].

Considerable in-depth research on this danger has been undertaken by Dr
Mary Pillai and Professor Gisli Gudjonsson.[2]

This is not fiction, although to those who have not suffered the reality of
the stories that follow they will seem so improbable as to be unacceptable as
fiction. It will seem even more improbable that this could happen to a happy
father or mother, grandfather or grandmother, comfortable in the knowledge
that they have always done their best by their children (although admitting
to the inevitable mistakes of parenthood), loved and cared for them and
would lay down their lives for them.

Imagine that you are resting comfortably at home when the telephone rings
or you receive an e-mail or letter, or a visit from your son or daughter or,
most traumatic of all, answer the door to a social worker or to the police who
ask you to accompany them to the police station to answer certain allegations
that have been made against you. You may or may not be aware that your
son or daughter has been experiencing problems to do with marriage, school,
work or personal relationships. It may be that they are unhappy because, as
one psychotherapist put it, '*they are unable to accept that life is hard as well
as beautiful,*' or their passage through puberty has been more traumatic than
usual, or they are wrestling with their sexuality or, quite simply, they are
dissatisfied with their life. You may or may not know that they have sought
help from one of more than 450 types of therapy available today. Or you
may even, naively, have suggested this yourself or acquiesced to advice from a
headmaster or practice nurse that your son or daughter should seek therapy.
It may be that your son or daughter has no problems but has responded to
peer pressure to acquire the latest 'must have' of counselling. The foregoing
is the starting point for most of the stories that follow.

Professor Weiskrantz's analogy, on page 34, 'these are compound fractures
that may never heal' accurately describes the long-term effect of recovered
memory therapy. Where the problem is kept within the family unit, there is
hope of a measure of reconciliation, although numerous case histories show
that the scars never fully heal. However, where the allegations are followed
by police intervention, public humiliation and possible imprisonment, the
sense of injustice and bitterness felt by the wrongly accused and the feelings
of guilt (if admitted) by the accuser can make any hope of a return to normal
family relationships impossible.

Part III.

The justice system's dilemma: legal issues

Introduction to Part III

Given that practitioners and social workers are required by law to notify the authorities when they suspect they have evidence of child abuse, the inevitable consequence of the beliefs and practices described in the preceding Part is the involvement of the police and courts. This Part, therefore, aims to show how ignorance by many in the legal system of the complexities and unreliability of memory, coupled with an understandable anxiety to protect those, particularly children, who are abused, has prejudiced the rights of the defendant, leading to the tragedies related in Part IV.

'The stuff of nightmares'

A car stopped opposite our drive today. It was very sleek, a long black Volvo, with black glass windows. It rested there. I have heard from our own members so often, of cars which park, wait and watch. Then the occupants emerge, ring at a bell and eventually an ageing man is escorted away — to a police station, questioning, maybe a charge of historic sexual abuse, bail, and eventually a trial, often imprisonment, innocent or not.

Eight years ago, not long after I was accused by my younger daughter, then in her thirties, I saw a car pull up outside my house. The driver waited. I could not bear the suspense. He looked like a plain clothes policeman. I went out to him, asked what he was doing.

He was a cab driver, taking my neighbour to Heathrow ...

Years later, whenever a mysterious car silently draws up and an unknown occupant just waits, the nightmare begins again. Am I going to have to find the address of a solicitor? Have we got months of hell looming as I try to prove my innocence of allegations stretching back more than 30 years? It's happened to so many others.

(An accused father)

(BFMS Forum 2009)

10. A barrister's view: rights, risks and responsibilities

The following is the text of a short speech by Barrister Pamela Radcliffe given at the launch of the BFMS booklet Fractured families *at the House of Lords in May 2007 and revised in 2009.*

I am going to focus on rights, risks and responsibilities. Firstly I am concerned with the rights, the right to a fair trial and the right not to be wrongly convicted. In February 2003 the Lord Chief Justice, Lord Woolf, in the case of *Regina v Brian Selwyn B* famously stated that:

> At the heart of our criminal justice system is the principle that while it is important that justice is done to the victim, in the final analysis the fact remains that it is even more important that an injustice is not done to the defendant. It is central to the way we administer justice in this country that although it may mean that some guilty people go unpunished it is more important that the innocent are not wrongly convicted.

There is no perfect criminal justice system. Miscarriages of justice and wrongful convictions will statistically always occur. However, it is the duty of the judges and the practitioners to ensure that from start to finish the trial process minimises the chances of injustice occurring. There is increasing tension between balancing the rights of the accuser against the competing right of the defendant to receive a fair trial.

Since the abolition of the 1956 Sexual Offences Act corroboration requirement in sexual offences, legislation and case law have resulted, some would say, in an imbalance tipped in favour of the accuser, particularly where historical sexual allegations are concerned. We are talking of an increasing number of allegations being made that go back twenty or more years. It is now exceedingly difficult to mount a successful abuse of process argument based upon the prejudice caused by this delay. Typically in these cases vital documents that may have disproved the allegation on a material point have been lost. Potentially helpful witnesses are dead. Details of the allegations may be vague and extremely difficult for the defendant to counter, other than saying simply, 'I didn't do it. Nothing happened like that.'

Some would say that a fair trial in these circumstances is well-nigh impossible. Well, where does that leave us in relation to the particular issue that the BFMS is interested in, recovered memories? Researcher and academic Richard Ofshe at the University of California, is reported as saying of recovered memory, that it is either the most fascinating psychological discovery of the 20th century or the centrepiece of the most embarrassing mistake modern psychiatry and psychotherapy have ever made.

In 2000 Pope, Oliva and Hudson conducted a review of the studies of psychological symptoms in trauma survivors. Of the 11,000 victims in these studies none reported having amnesia of the prime traumatic event. The victims in these retrospective studies included a whole spectrum of trauma, ranging from holocaust and war victims to explosions, natural disasters and rape victims. However, in spite of the 'Brandon' report, in spite of extensive research on memory by Professor Loftus[1] and others, the debate about the validity of recovered memories is as vociferous and divided as ever.

Criminal allegations are arising from this new species of evidence. That is what I am calling it. It is not evidence spontaneously recalled by a complainant in the traditional way. The evidence is 'memories' that have been reportedly recovered via memory work. These 'memories' may have taken months or years to emerge via different therapeutic methods. The interviews or sessions in which these 'memories' have emerged will not have been recorded by the therapist other than in sketchy notes. The way in which the memory emerged will not be transparent and cannot be subjected to scientific scrutiny or even analysis.

The risks to the fairness of the trial process are compounded in recovered memory cases. In addition to all the usual problems associated with historical allegations, the jury is confronted with a witness who may present in a very convincing manner. Added to that is the social and psychological pressures that jurors may feel, that is the natural desire to empathise with the complainant.

The prosecution address the jury from the outset on the basis that the witness is truthful and reliable.

The jury are not aware of the defence case unless it is spelt out in the police interview, which in turn may or may not have been drawn to their attention at the outset. Therefore, the jury approach the complainant's evidence in chief unaware of how to approach her evidence, other than via common sense.

This traditional approach in my view tilts the trial process from the outset in favour of the Crown. I pose whether we should be considering the introduction of a defence speech after the Crown's opening which would fully and fairly set the scene for the evidence to be heard, from the defence viewpoint.

The direct risk posed to the fairness of the trial by recovered memory evidence is that potentially unreliable evidence is automatically admitted in evidence and presumed to be reliable and presented as being reliable, until or unless the defence attack it.

This generally passive approach of the Crown is in direct contrast to that of the defence who have to be proactive in these cases, investigating the background circumstances which generate a complaint via the disclosure process.

We come therefore to the third part which is the responsibility of the investigators, advocates and judges. In my opinion, cases of historical sexual allegations, where there is no independent corroboration of the allegations or proof that they occurred, give rise to extra burdens and responsibilities and call for extra caution by all those who play a role in the criminal justice system.

What needs to be done

The consequences of sexual allegations start to flow from the moment the complaint is made. I highlight particular issues ... Firstly, regarding the sufficiency and reliability of evidence called by the prosecution. All historical sexual allegations should be subject to an effective and real preliminary investigation prior to any charging of a defendant. There is an existing duty on the investigator and the Crown prosecutor, to be independent, fair and objective and to conduct a proper investigation prior to charging the accused. The Code for the Crown Prosecutors [2010] actually states in terms: *'When deciding whether there is sufficient evidence to prosecute, prosecutors must consider whether the evidence can be used and whether it is reliable'*[2] (paragraph 4.7). This Code needs to be scrupulously followed.

The investigator should, in my opinion, examine historical complaints carefully from the outset. He should explore how the complaint came to be made, whether there was psychological counselling or any mental health issues and if so whether this impacts on the reliability of the complaint, prior to the charge, not afterwards in the course of late disclosure, or just prior to trial.

I query whether there should be specially trained police officers and Crown Prosecutors for historical sexual allegations or for an independent mental health professional to review the evidence at the outset and assist with the assessment of the strength of the case at the pre-charge stage. If the prosecution were conducted in this way, in my opinion, the weakest cases could immediately be identified and discontinued.

The trial process: there are two crucial issues to address, in relation to admissibility and reliability. It is arguable that where recovered memories have been generated by therapy, there should be a pre-trial judicial determination on admissibility, following an evaluation of reliability of memory evidence. It should be for the prosecution to prove reliability. In my opinion the current traditional approach whereby the defence reacts to the evidence amounts effectively to a reversal of the burden of proof. It is not for the defence to prove that these memories or pseudo memories are false. It is for the Crown to prove at the outset that the memories are capable of being reliable to the essential criminal standard. This approach would enable the judge to act as a gateway whereby he could exclude from the outset inherently unreliable evidence. This may result in the halting of the trial at this stage. What would this entail? Reviewing all the therapeutic methods used and an assessment of the professional efficacy and underlying scientific methodology of the therapeutic process used. It would not entail hearing from the complainant.

If the underlying therapeutic process is flawed, then logically, the evidence which emanates from it must be equally contaminated and flawed. In medical science today the emphasis is on evidence-based medicine. The variety of psychological methods being used in memory work need to be open to scrutiny and critical assessment and proved to be reliable. This approach is not novel and is consistent with the presumption of innocence and the right to a fair trial.

What criteria should the judge use? In my submission the time is now ripe for the Daubert[3] criteria to be looked at again to see whether they should be applied in our legal system. Daubert is an American case. The judge looks at the evidence and assesses:

   i. whether the expert's technique or theory can be or has been tested, that is, whether the expert's theory can be challenged in some objective sense, or whether it is instead simply a subjective, conclusory approach that cannot be reasonably assessed for reliability

   ii. whether the technique or theory has been subject to peer review and publication

   iii. the known or potential rate of error of the technique of theory when applied

   iv. the existence and maintenance of standards and controls and

   v. whether the technique or theory has been generally accepted in the scientific community.

The Court of Appeal has so far resisted attempts to introduce the Daubert tests. However it may be that in the wake of high profile miscarriages of justice involving medical evidence the time is ripe to reassess and review.

Conclusion

The so called 'memory wars' linger on with as much fervour as ever. Recovered memories are not scientifically verifiable. The theories generating them are not subject to empirical investigation. 'Memory work' involves repeated sessions, typically over a long period of time, with the gradual evolution of vague thoughts and ideas developing into fully-fledged allegations. This is happening today. Cases are still coming up, twelve years after the 'Brandon' Report.

Is the legal profession aware of the extent of concerned division within the mental health field? I fear not. Is it good enough to leave evidence generated by this means and subject to professional dissent amongst the medical profession, to the jury? Surely not. I believe that allegations such as these may put justice in jeopardy. It is unclear how many recovered memory cases are proceeding to trial and I cannot give you any official statistics on the conviction/acquittal rate.

Whilst recovered memory evidence may form a small proportion of sexual complaints as a whole, the potential for miscarriages of justice to occur is real and the consequence of such miscarriages, as you know, are catastrophic. I know I am preaching to the converted but I leave you with this: the untimely death of Sally Clark should make us redouble our efforts to prevent unreliable experts' evidence shattering any more lives and I leave you with a quote:

> The desire to convict the guilty must never be allowed to increase
> the risk of convicting the innocent.

11. An expert witness's view: does 'recovered' memory have a place in the legal system?

The following article, by Dr Janet Boakes, FRCPsych was first published in the BFMS Newsletter October 2005. The article was written in the wake of the controversy concerning the role of expert witnesses Professor Meadow and Dr Camille San Lazaro and revised in 2009. Dr Boakes is a retired Consultant psychiatrist and was co-author of the 'Brandon' report.

In July 2005 Professor Sir Roy Meadow was struck off the Medical Register following his appearance in the conviction of Sally Clark, sending shock waves through the ranks of potential medical expert witnesses. Although his subsequent appeal was upheld and his name restored to the register, the Court of Appeal overturned the High Court's decision that expert witnesses should be immune from referral to their regulatory bodies' disciplinary hearings. As a result, aspiring medical experts, especially child psychiatrists and paediatricians, became wary of giving expert evidence causing fears for the effect on child protection work.

The medical expert witness appears in criminal, civil and family courts. His role is to advise the court on particular issues that fall within his knowledge and experience and that may be outside the common experience of members of the jury. The limitations of memory, the dangers posed by suggestion, and the whole debate around repression, recovered memories and the false memory syndrome are amongst those issues.

Our judicial system is an adversarial rather than inquisitorial one. It is more concerned with the strength of rival arguments presented by the opposing parties than it is with discerning the truth. Within this adversarial system the expert witness, although called by one of the opposing parties, owes his first duty to the court and must remain independent and impartial. He is not there to advocate for his particular team but to assist the Court achieve the overriding objective, that cases be dealt with justly, although it is in the nature of events that the expert is first instructed in the hope that his evidence will support the side that instructs him. Because of the adversarial nature of our system, the expert can expect to be cross examined, sometimes rigorously, and may be opposed by an expert who will present a contrary view.

The expert witness differs from the ordinary witness to fact. A fact witness can only testify to what he has experienced for himself. An expert is allowed to base his opinion upon all the available information, drawing upon his professional knowledge and experience. The psychiatric expert is qualified by knowledge, training and experience to give an opinion on psychiatric issues in order to assist the court about matters that are unlikely to fall within the experience of the jury. As an independent witness, he will not be the treating doctor, who would be called as a professional witness and, like any other witness as to fact, would speak from his personal knowledge of the patient.

Any expert evidence which advances a novel scientific theory or technique should be subjected to special scrutiny to determine whether it meets a basic level of reliability. This is of course the nub of the matter in historical allegations of sexual abuse where the theory of repressed and recovered memories is advanced.

In the USA the Daubert standard sets out four criteria for determining whether expert testimony constitutes scientific knowledge.

- Can the theory be/has it been tested? (can it be falsified?)

- What is the potential or known rate of error?

- Has the theory been subjected to peer review and publication?

- Has the theory gained acceptance in the academic and scientific community?

There is no such standard in the UK; the closest we come is the Bolam Test which holds that a doctor is not negligent if he has acted in accordance with a practice accepted as proper by a responsible body of medical men skilled in that particular art — even if there is a body of opinion which would take a contrary view. Nevertheless the expert can be expected to apply the same intellectual rigour to his testimony as he would in other fields and to justify his conclusions to the Court. It is important not to stray beyond one's area of expertise, as for example Professor Meadow, when he testified about statistics in the Sally Clark case, and found himself before the GMC on a charge of serious professional misconduct.

What makes an expert?

In the UK there are no minimum standards that must be met by aspiring experts. Anyone can declare himself to be an expert. All that is needed is some practical experience or a professional qualification. One expert in a historical sex abuse case was a therapist who described herself as 'working with different worlds and different levels,' leaving judge and jury somewhat baffled. She had a professional qualification and experience, but no knowledge of memory, psychology, mental illness or the relevant research literature.

It is the judge alone who decides who is an expert and whether or not to allow the inclusion of expert testimony. Some judges will admit psychiatric evidence in historic sexual abuse allegations only to show that the accuser had a recognised mental illness at the time an allegation was made, and will exclude information that points to an iatrogenic condition, arising for instance from therapy or counselling. They regard this as within the capability of the jury to determine. It is rare, in my experience, for there to be clear signs of formal mental illness in these cases. Most false allegations occur in people who are anxious and depressed and seeking explanations for why their lives have gone wrong. One case in which I gave evidence was unusual in that I was able to show, from the medical records, clear evidence of paranoid beliefs, delusions and hallucinations that directly preceded the first allegations. This is exceptional and more usually the expert will want to review competing hypotheses to explain how someone may come to make delayed allegations of sexual abuse, why the testimony of an accuser may have changed over time, or how any symptoms may have come about.

Judges dislike the battle of experts and, believing that most matters can be decided by a jury using its collective common sense, would prefer not to allow the expert into court. Lord Justice Judge held, 'if the outcome of a criminal trial depends on the serious disagreement between reputable experts, it will be unwise, and therefore unsafe, for the prosecution to proceed.' In one case in which I was instructed, my report was so much at variance with that of the Crown's expert that the judge declared, 'If even the experts cannot agree, how can we expect the jury to do so?' and stayed the case. Some judges restrict what can be admitted, allowing evidence about how memory works, but excluding evidence about the role of suggestion and external influence; others choose to hear evidence in a *voir dire* (preliminary hearing) before deciding on its admissibility.

Expert evidence

Broadly we might divide the expert into one of three types. The scientific expert will be called to educate the court on the relevant scientific literature. In cases of historical allegations of sexual abuse this will probably cover the science of memory and of suggestion; it may also cover theories of repression and dissociation, 'recovered memory' and the 'false memory syndrome.'

The second type of expert may be called as much for his clinical expertise as for his familiarity with the scientific literature. He will wish to review any medical records and give an opinion on the presence or absence of formal mental illness in the accuser that might affect the testimony given. A history of psychiatric illness does not automatically make an allegation untrue and the medical expert can help to tease out the development of the allegation vis-à-vis any illness and determine if mental disorder has contributed to the allegations being false, or is an incidental finding that does not challenge the reliability of the accuser. An expert is not allowed to state an opinion about whether or not the accuser is telling the truth, which is for the jury, but can give an opinion on whether credibility or reliability are undermined by internal or external factors, such as mental illness or, for example, counselling.

The third expert is one who acts as a consultant, assisting the legal team to understand the psychiatric aspects but not necessarily being called to give evidence. These roles are not discrete and may easily elide with each other.

What does the future hold?

In today's complex and technical society the need for experts to assist the Court is unlikely to disappear, although, in keeping with so many other areas, it will probably be hedged about with restrictions. It is likely that there will be increasing calls for training, accreditation and monitoring and some professionals have advocated the introduction of a Code of Practice for experts.

Without the support of expert witnesses some people, both the innocent accused and the genuine victim, may be left as a victim of the system. Yet there are increasing pressures on potential expert witnesses. Following the referral of Professor Meadow to the GMC, medical experts are wary of becoming involved. Acting as an expert witness is already time-consuming, laborious and stressful, without the added worry of ending up before one's disciplinary body. Constraints on the Legal Aid budget limit what can be paid and can sometimes make finding an expert problematic. In the Civil Courts there has been a shift to appointing a single joint expert, and it is likely this may be extended to the criminal courts in due course. While this may save money, there are concerns that in some cases a defendant may be barred from an effective challenge to a controversial opinion.

12. A solicitor's view: can symptoms be evidence?

The solicitor writing here argues that current adult psychiatric illness in an accuser cannot be used by the prosecution as 'postdictive evidence' of experience of abuse in childhood. The solicitor assisted as a family member in the Swan case, but not as his legal representative. The name 'Edward Swan' is a pseudonym as is 'Michael Brown.' The law requires that Michael Brown be never identified, though Edward Swan, as the accused proven innocent, can be.

When the police came to arrest him in early 2007, retired civil servant Edward Swan was 81 years old and had been married for 53 years. He had three children and nine grandchildren. He was a man of exemplary character with a background of voluntary service to his church and community, including some forty years as a youth leader and Sunday school teacher. He was now in frail health, had poor hearing and had difficulty walking without crutches.

Edward Swan was arrested in front of his family, taken to a police detention centre and questioned at length over the course of a day. As he discovered, at the end of 2006 a 34 year old man, Michael Brown, recently discharged from a psychiatric hospital and still suffering from a serious mental illness, had made a complaint to the police that he had been indecently assaulted by Edward Swan on more than 145 occasions over a period of nearly four years commencing in the spring of 1987. Brown said he had made the complaint at the suggestion of his psychotherapist so that he could 'find closure.'

Swan denied all the accusations and said that nothing of the sort had ever happened. Brown had been a pupil in Edward Swan's Sunday school class until September 1986 and had visited Mr and Mrs Swan regularly in their home between 1988 and 1990 where he had helped with gardening in return for pocket money. This arrangement was at the request of Brown's parents. During 1989, the Swans had become disturbed by Brown developing very odd and intrusive behaviour. In December 1989 they had suggested that he spend more time with his own family. Brown's reaction was explosive with a fit of shaking rage as if he had been betrayed by the Swans. The Swans saw relatively little of him after this and soon after Brown got a job and moved away from the area.

Edward Swan was released on bail and there then followed a year-long investigation leading to him standing trial on eight charges under the Sexual Offences Act 1956. What was puzzling to the Swan family was why the police and the CPS were proceeding when their only evidence seemed to be based on the uncorroborated word of one person. The Code for Crown Prosecutors requires that cases should only be brought if there is a better than even chance of conviction. Yet there was really just the accuser's word against the defendant's.

Though mental patients should never be denied access to the justice system, at the same time some notice should have been taken that the accusations might have arisen as confabulations from the accuser's mental illness. Instead, as became apparent from the documents disclosed pre-trial by the prosecution, the police and the CPS were anxious to build a case that the accuser's mental illness, in itself, was evidence.

The first, and most obvious, dilemma for the justice system is that by their very nature sexual offences are committed in private. There are very rarely witnesses. Immediate disclosure may produce corroborative forensic evidence, but that may not, in itself, be conclusive of guilt. When, as in the Swan case, the allegations are about events supposed to have occurred twenty years previously, there is a very low probability of establishing any reliable corroboration. In practice, then, a charge under the Sexual Offences Act can be carried forward as one person's word against another's but only if the accuser is likely to make a more convincing and coherent witness than the defendant.

A further dilemma is that a genuine traumatised victim may prove a poor witness, whereas a glib sex criminal may provide a believable false account. Conversely, an accuser primed with false memories may present a vehement and vivid account against an innocent defendant whose bewildered denial may seem thin in contrast.

The first recourse of the police is to seek other accusations. The process is known as 'trawling.' In sexual offence cases, it can provide effective corroboration if a defendant faces multiple credible accusations from adults. The genuine rapist or child sex abuser often displays a persistent pattern of crime that is only revealed by 'trawling' operations.

However, 'trawling' has dangers for the justice system. It may create multiple accusations that appear independent, but which are in common prompted by greed, malice or revenge. Whilst such motivations can be identified, a potentially devastating problem for an innocent defendant is the 'sibling domino' where an initial accusation of incestuous sexual abuse is followed by another accusation from a sibling arising from 'trawling.' This may be prompted by sibling solidarity, or, more problematically, as a by-product of 'cognitive dissonance' where, in seeking to come to terms with a loved and trusted sibling making vile accusations against a loved and trusted parent, the second sibling is introduced to the same poor-quality psychotherapy or toxic self-help regime that generated the first accusation. Fortunately for Edward Swan, 'trawling' produced no false corroboration. To the contrary, a number of those contacted rang the Swans to express indignation and some later gave evidence for the defence.

The second recourse of the police, given lack of other evidence in this type of case, is to secure an admission of guilt during interrogation or, failing that, to secure self-incriminating statements. Some thirty years ago, a surprising proportion of people accused of sexual offences would break down, confess guilt and express remorse when confronted with their crimes. In the case of incest, the confession rate was over 90%. However, as accusations of childhood sexual abuse mushroomed in the 1980's and 1990's, the confession rate fell. Edward Swan emphatically denied the accusations. What then followed was a classic example of why solicitors may urge clients to exercise their right to silence. Because he had nothing to hide, Edward Swan freely answered all questions. Though the police should have been considering these innocent explanations, it became clear that what they were, in fact, doing was building a case.

An example of this was Brown's claim that Edward Swan 'carried a picture of him around in his wallet.' The innocent explanation was that Swan had once taken a picture of each boy in his class on a Sunday School outing, had had them in an envelope in his pocket for a few days in order to give them to the respective parents at church as a souvenir. Brown's picture had been given to his mother who had expressed her thanks. Yet, at the subsequent trial the prosecution made much of this, claiming it as an 'admission' and evidence of homosexual infatuation with Brown.

Of the eight charges Edward Swan faced, three referred to specific alleged instances and he was able at trial to prove they were false. But five of the charges were general catch-all 'Between January 1st and December 31st . . .' allegations. Whilst it may be possible to refute specific instance charges by proving that they could not have taken place, it is extraordinarily difficult to so refute general catch-all charges from a period so long ago.

Though Mr and Mrs Swan were profoundly shocked as to why the Crown Prosecution Service was proceeding, with the charges came disclosure of prosecution documents. These included some thirty pages of statement and attachments from Brown plus correspondence from his psychotherapist. This proved invaluable in explaining Brown's motivation and the CPS strategy. Brown blamed his mental illness, Obsessive-Compulsive Disorder (OCD), on the 'childhood sexual abuse he had suffered.' The CPS was seeking to introduce this as evidence.

In US TV cop shows, the police and district attorneys have instant access to authoritative psychiatric and medical expertise. Not so in real life in the UK. In the Swan case, Brown, the investigating policeman and Brown's psychotherapist met together in February 2007 in what the psychotherapist called 'a case discussion meeting.' Questions posed by the Crown Prosecution Service included, 'Is there an expert who can say with certainty that OCD arose as a result of the child abuse?' Questions related to the cause of Brown's mental illness, the 'quality of the witness' and disposing of 'false memory syndrome' as an argument were also raised. Remember that these questions were not being put to an independent adviser but to Brown's psychotherapist in front of Brown.

Whether Brown's psychotherapist was arrogant or just gullible cannot be determined. Certain phrases in Brown's statements seem derived from Internet material and it is likely that he fed her exactly what he knew she would be looking for. In any event, she swallowed the sex abuse story hook, line and sinker and regurgitated it as if it were proven fact.

OCD is a common condition affecting some 600,000 people in the UK alone.[1] The effects can be severe and debilitating. The cause is unknown but onset is often linked to major life events such as puberty and bereavement. In researching Edward Swan's defence, it was found that, despite the prevalence of OCD, there was not one case in the medical literature linking OCD onset to childhood sexual abuse. Michael Brown would have been a unique case. Despite the unlikelihood of this, Brown's psychotherapist did not alert the police. Nor did she point out a rather obvious possibility — that the accusations arose from Brown's illness rather than being evidence that he had been abused. A substantial proportion of OCD patients suffer from obsessive thoughts and images. These can be repetitive, vivid and disturbing and may involve violent, sexual or blasphemous thoughts and images. The dull, repetitive sex acts Brown described in his statement would fit the bill as imaginary OCD obsessions very well. His odd behaviour in 1989, his taking excessively long showers and endlessly fiddling with his hair would also be good indicators for early-onset OCD. Additionally, a common symptom of OCD is the making of false confessions and seeking the permission of others for the patient to be the way he or she is. This also fits Brown's history of revelation and therapy.

Brown had a history of passing through the hands of various counsellors and therapy programmes before ending up as an in-patient at a psychiatric hospital. There was no way Brown's psychotherapist could have assessed whether his memories were 'recovered' or not, real or false. She said in her report to the police that he volunteered the abuse details at their first meeting and spoke about them freely. However, that is no indicator of likely truth — rather the contrary. Real victims of sex abuse do not happily volunteer such information to strangers. Brown had been telling and elaborating this story for some ten years, receiving sympathy and support from all he told it to. Above all, it gave him someone to blame for his mental illness — it was not his fault.

The psychotherapist also diagnosed mild Post Traumatic Stress Disorder arising from 'the abuse.' Yet PTSD Syndrome, though a very real mental disorder, is no proof that the patient has undergone a real trauma. In America, one veteran suffered so severely over the years from PTSD arising from his capture and torture by the Viet Cong that he eventually committed suicide. It was only later that his widow discovered he had never been to Vietnam. One million Americans were treated for full-blown PTSD arising from their combat experiences in Vietnam, yet fewer than 300,000 Americans actually saw combat there.

With the evidentiary dilemmas that the justice system faces in dealing with accusations of sexual abuse in the far past, it is perhaps understandable why the CPS seized upon Brown's proffered psychiatric symptoms as potential evidence. This is known as 'postdictive analysis.' A child who has suffered real sexual abuse may go on to develop a range of psychiatric symptoms, usually related to anxiety disorders, as an adult. That is 'predictive.' However, most sexually abused children, thankfully, go on to lead happy normal lives as adults. Many adults who had perfectly normal childhoods develop psychiatric symptoms of anxiety disorders. So 'postdictive analysis' really has no validity in law or in psychiatry. You cannot presume, because someone has certain psychiatric symptoms, that anything real has actually happened to them in the past.

Of course, it would be perverse for a defendant to claim that a severely traumatised rape victim was an unreliable witness because he or she was traumatised. That is akin to the apocryphal murderer who killed his parents and then asked for leniency on the grounds that he was an orphan. But there is a big difference between issues relating to the reliability of a witness in a recent sexual allegation and postdictive analysis of the psychiatric ailments of someone who alleges an offence committed many years before.

As the Swan trial date neared, both prosecution and defence had problems with the psychiatric evidence. A jury only needs expert testimony on matters outside its normal range of experience. Brown's psychotherapist obviously saw herself as a potential expert witness. The defence, on the other hand, saw her as a culpable participant in Brown's creation of a wicked falsehood. To discredit her evidence it would be necessary to shred her reputation. Whilst that would not have been difficult, given the circumstances of the case, it would have taken time and 'there would be blood on the courtroom floor.' The jury would sit there, effectively, as spectators as the psychotherapist was demolished. They would still be asking the question 'did the defendant do it or not?'

In the event, the prosecution and the defence reached an informal agreement. The postdictive psychiatric claims would not be presented by the prosecution and the defence would not attack the credibility of the prosecution witness solely on the grounds that he was mentally ill. The defence was hampered by not being able to explain the accusation in terms of the prosecution witness' mental illness but gained from not having the key issues obfuscated by pseudo-science presented as evidence.

At trial, Michael Brown had a comfortable presentation as the prosecution took him through his accusations. However, when the defence barrister cross-examined, the jury saw an extraordinary disintegration. Brown had told his story over the years, adding, elaborating and embellishing and had always been met with sympathy. This was probably the first time his story had ever been challenged and Brown had got his time frame wrong. Because he had fabricated the mass of detail to fit what he thought was the time frame, his story unravelled. Incontrovertible evidence proved the first alleged offence could not have taken place in 1987. The earliest it could have happened was May 1988. Brown was therefore not as young as he said he was when the first offence was alleged. Furthermore, the remaining 144 allegations had to be squashed into little more than 18 months. He would have had to have been sexually abused some two or three times on virtually every afternoon he visited. This in a busy house with the defendant's wife and other family members present. As Brown's account fell apart, the judge instructed the jury three times to return directed Not Guilty verdicts. The jury then found Edward Swan Not Guilty on the five remaining charges.

Subsequently, after receipt of a complaint, the police declined to prosecute Brown on a charge that he had sought to pervert the course of justice and the Crown Prosecution Service rejected a formal complaint that they had not followed the Code for Crown Prosecutors.

A conclusion from the Swan case is that the police and Crown Prosecution Service are lamentably ill-informed about mental illnesses. There is an official code of practice they must follow where the defendant is mentally ill, but there is no code of practice to evaluate complainants and witnesses who are mentally ill or emotionally disturbed. A persistent attitude taken by the police is, 'Why would this person bring such an accusation unless it was true?' It may also be the attitude of jury members, which is very dangerous for the justice system if false memories and motivations arising from mental disturbance cannot be presented as explanation where relevant. Additionally, the mentally ill people the police usually encounter in beat work tend to be extreme cases — unfortunate confused street-dwellers or deranged and sometimes dangerous people. Where a mentally ill person seems quite rational and normal to talk to, a policeman untrained in mental health issues may have no frame of reference to judge the reliability of a statement based on a deep delusion unless it is overtly preposterous, such as sexual abuse during alien abduction. And even overtly preposterous statements can be taken seriously, as the 'satanic ritual' prosecutions of the 1980's and early 1990s demonstrated [Inquiry into the Removal of Children from Orkney in February 1991, 1992, La Fontaine, 1994, 1997].

The Swan case also demonstrated the weakness of police procedure. Independent psychiatric advisers were not used. The police went to Brown's own psychotherapist with Brown in attendance. They were referred by her to a colleague who confirmed everything she said, including the assumption that the 'sex abuse' was a matter of fact. The colleague interviewed Brown briefly, but, really, this is not enough to establish any authoritative opinion. Mental illness is not like physical illness. Mental patients can be both deceptive and self-deceiving and it may take many sessions over several months to establish a reliable diagnosis. Above all, the police and CPS were clearly not seeking to establish a balanced view to reach a judgment. Their questions centred on building a case against Edward Swan.

The dilemmas of the justice system in dealing with accusations of historic sexual abuse stretch far beyond the immediacies of evidence procurement. There are political factors such as the desire to raise the conviction rate for rape and similar sexual offences. There may also be a frustration factor where police and prosecutors, unable to bring contemporaneous child sex abuse prosecutions because of the fragility of some child witnesses, seize upon a historic case because the witness is an adult. However, the real lesson of the Swan case is that an inordinate amount of police and court time was spent pursuing an ill-founded prosecution based on the sexual obsessions of a mentally ill man and his gullible psychotherapist — time that could have been better spent investigating and prosecuting real offences.

13. An accused's view of the legal system

'E' whose case is described in chapter 23

The two years that have elapsed since the case against me was withdrawn have been a period of highs and lows, some very deep troughs, but it has been also a time for further profound searching and reflection.

After the initial relief of finally being freed from the charges came the emotional tidal wave.

The various emotions surging through my mind range from anger and frustration, disbelief and cynicism, through to bitterness and regret. I will deal with each in turn.

Anger and frustration

At a system that is unable and/or unwilling to accept that present day difficulties in an adult may not result from fictional claims of childhood abuse and there may well be current clinical reasons for these problems. Occasionally there may be no explanation for the condition.

That there is an institutional prejudice against believing that parents will do their absolute best to raise a difficult child with behavioural problems, while the professions have been reluctant to recognise their own lack of expertise in offering remedial assistance where a child has mental health problems — or to be objective and open minded as to the causes.

At a legal system, often too cosy with the prosecution, that readily accepts arguments for a *'prima facie'* case and is then blind and indifferent to the humiliation of many accused who are then acquitted because of actual *lack* of evidence. But the system never apologises for mistakes.

That in recovered memory cases the police have been thrust from the outset into a situation for which their basic investigative techniques are inadequate. Police are not skilled in the psychiatric/psychological approach that is so desperately required in the initial stages of recovered memory investigations.

At a system of investigation which fails to protect the innocent. When was the cornerstone of British justice that it is better that ten guilty men go free than one innocent man is convicted removed without public discussion or outcry? Have we returned to the belief so prevalent in less 'enlightened' times when the belief in legal circles and judiciary that one would not be brought before a court if one had not done wrong and if before the court one must be guilty?

(This sweeping statement may appear at first reading as a bitter reaction to charges falsely brought but it is a remark often made within 'judicial' circles and deeply held and embedded by many within our society at large. [The knowledge of an insider.])

That despite the claims of politicians, procedures are loaded against the innocent. Complaints of alleged abuse are accepted at first instance as genuine, with little or no impartial investigation. Then, if a second 'victim' is found this is then taken as absolute corroboration and a '*prima facie*' case for a prosecution is believed to exist. If the defendant says that lengthy involvement with mental health professionals has influenced the accuser this is discounted as 'covering his tracks' — if it is registered at all.

That allegations go back in some cases many decades which makes it almost impossible to interview witnesses, locate establishments or records. Tracing relatives, professionals, neighbours and friends, some long-since deceased, is virtually impossible as is expecting people to have clear detailed recollections of the lives of another family 20, 30 or 40 years later.

At having to conduct an investigation one would believe the police would have undertaken and to do it with only the very limited resources of a private citizen and local solicitor — and to explain to all why and how one is acting as a Private Investigator, seeking information on a purely goodwill basis. We learned that necessity is a speedy tutor in developing detection and investigative skills.

Then there is disbelief . . .

That — after the shock of the charges subsided — we should have arrived at this situation, when all the facts were out there in the public domain, in the many contemporary records held by public bodies such as the Local Authority, Health Authority, and Education Authority etc. After all, we reasoned, all that was required of the police was to locate these records, speak to some of the professionals still alive, and they would quickly understand there could be no validity in these claims of abuse.

... and cynicism

This reaction — and it can't be good for society at large — was a result of challenging the police officers as to why they had not carried out the basic checks. We realised these officials were not interested in the truth; they wanted the scalp of a minor public official to parade in the canteen. This realisation was later borne out from comments recalled by their colleagues in private. Now when we hear or see reports, not just of alleged acts of abuse, but other cases, the thought intervenes: 'Who is being fitted up now?' Is evidence which would clear them being excluded? Is truth not a consideration?

There is cynicism too, when the system is unable to admit 'we got it wrong' or apologise, when extensive searches and enquiries have revealed nothing supporting the case in question.

And while there are predators at large in our society who prey on women and children for their own sexual gratification, there are those who also prey on the vulnerable to further their own cause or beliefs. Good examples are the advocates of 'recovered memory,' the therapists who will 'assist' and manipulate the vulnerable in order to maximise their careers and reputation. To these so-called professionals the plight of those falsely accused of truly heinous crimes are of no concern. After all, these usually good and caring parents or relatives have to be seen as 'perverts.' The thought that their own beliefs and theories are erroneous simply must not occur to them, nor the devastation these professionals leave in their wake as they move on.

Finally, I will add the feeling of vulnerability in that at any moment anyone now has the opportunity to make an allegation reaching back decades and, because of the way in which our laws are now constructed and interpreted, such a complaint will be investigated and usually believed, as if it had been committed yesterday. It is thought, with phony reasonability, why would someone make such allegations if they are false? We unfortunately know differently.

Another legacy of this situation is that youngsters now know they can cause difficulties for any person who challenges them or they dislike. For example, a pensioner who shouted at a group stoning geese and ducks on a canal was accused of assault by one boy. The old man was arrested and locked in a cell (I know the feeling) and eventually released.

Adults are now running scared of children and young people who know only too well that if they complain the system will swing into action to 'protect' them. What a mess.

Part IV.

Miscarriages of memory: police and CPS investigations, criminal trials, appeals and re-trials

Introduction to Part IV

The following case histories are largely — but not entirely — drawn from the BFMS's data base of 672[1] criminal cases in which the evidence was based wholly or partly on 'memories' allegedly recovered by a complainant while undergoing therapy and which led to investigation by the police or higher legal authority. In most cases the BFMS was asked to advise defendants and their legal teams, and to recommend expert witnesses. Other organisations are known to have advised defendants in similar cases.

Some of the cases did not proceed further than investigation by the police or CPS. However, while it is recognised that the police are required to act when an adult makes historic allegations of childhood abuse, where it is evident that the allegations have arisen out of therapy, an awareness by the police of the unreliability of the memory process might cause them to respond with a greater degree of caution. Dawn raids by teams of police and social workers on unsuspecting parents who are dragged off and held in police cells for lengthy questioning before all allegations are dropped (sometimes after a delay of many months while the case is considered by the Crown Prosecution Service), help no-one. It wastes police time and magnifies immensely the suffering of parents.

Reporting of many of these cases is severely restricted by *sub judice* or Family Court rules. For the same reasons, cases currently under investigation cannot be included.

Some of the cases are based on published court judgments and are in the public domain. Others are based on conversations with parents or written by the accused.

Further false memory case histories are recorded in *Fractured families* [Brand, 2007].

The following case histories are listed in reverse order according to the date of the latest legal or GMC involvement

14. *Sub judice* cases (2009/2010): the most recent cases we cannot report

During the latter stages in the preparation of this book, the BFMS was assisting defendants/appellants in a number of court cases which are subject to *sub judice* rules and/or family court restrictions.

These include four cases pending trial and three applying to the Criminal Cases Review Commission (CCRC) for an appeal.

15. 'A figment of the CPS's imagination?' (1999 to 2008)

This is one of the most recent and unusual court cases involving historical false allegations of childhood abuse. It concerned allegations made by two sisters that they had been abused by the husband of their older sister. It reached court late in 2008 when the jury, faced with glaring inconsistencies in the evidence placed before them, quickly returned a unanimous verdict of Not Guilty, following which the Judge, in a rare departure from convention, voiced before the open court her satisfaction with the outcome. Perhaps this was the Judge's way of admonishing the CPS for wasting their own and the court's time.

Notably the Judge, in her summing up, also drew attention to the fact that 30 years had elapsed since the abuse was alleged to have taken place. This had robbed the defendant of the opportunity of calling upon key defence witnesses who had since died. Furthermore, the claim that the 'memories' of abuse had been completely forgotten and only 'remembered' many years later while undergoing therapy, meant that forensic evidence and records of medical examinations did not exist. There was, therefore, no corroborative evidence. It was simply the defendant's word against that of the complainants.

Significantly, the jury were only away for 30 minutes on the final morning of the brief hearing before requesting clarification of one allegation, following which they found the defendant Not Guilty on all eight counts.

That the jury were able to dismiss so quickly the prosecution counsel's arguments in a case involving evidence reaching back nine years and of considerable complexity, raises important questions:

i. Why did the CPS pursue this court action when the weight of evidence was overwhelmingly in favour of the defendant — something that was very quickly obvious to the jury?

ii. Why did the prosecuting authorities decide not to interview the wife of the accused who would have been able to provide relevant background to the allegations by her younger sisters, particularly the long-term mental health problems of the youngest accuser, that might have avoided so much suffering?

iii. Did the CPS's decision to prosecute, perhaps, owe something to the point made by Pamela Radcliffe in chapter 10: 'Since the abolition of the 1956 Sexual Offences Act corroboration requirement in sexual offences, legislation and case law have resulted, some would say, in an imbalance tipped in favour of the accuser, particularly where historical sexual allegations are concerned.'

The case is, as already stated, unusual in a number of ways. But additionally it demonstrates the diverse origins of false memories. The background to the worsening relationship between the two accusing sisters-in-law of the defendant and the rest of the family dates back to 1999 although it reached a peak in 2006 at the time of the maternal mother's serious illness and death.

The younger of the two sisters had a long history of acute anorexia and had spent several periods undergoing psychiatric treatment in one of the country's foremost mental hospitals where she had been sectioned on three occasions. The older of the two had suffered from serious post natal depression and was known to have had marital difficulties. It appears that at no time during the lengthy treatment of the younger sister, which involved extensive psychotherapy, was there any hint of a background of childhood abuse, despite her later claims that she was abused by the defendant when she was five or six and also stalked by an unidentified married neighbour. Subsequently, during the trial, this aspect of her therapy was to play a significant part in the case for the defence.

The defendant picks up the story at the point in November 2006 when the two accusing sisters started therapy sessions during which they both maintained they had been abused in early childhood by their brother in law:

> The sessions went on throughout January, February and March 2007. When they had enough sessions/reports under their belts they reported the alleged abuse to the police.

> I got a phone call from the police round about mid-March 2007 and was asked to report to the police station to discuss the accusations made by the two complainants.

> I attended two more interviews under PACE (Police and Criminal Evidence Act) guidelines and was officially charged with the alleged abuse in August 2007. To make matters worse, I felt obliged to let my company know of the allegations, and based on these allegations, my boss decided that it may bring the name of the company into disrepute. I lost my job.

> I was summoned to appear at the Magistrates' Court on three occasions in total. On one of these appearances in particular the charges were read out in graphic detail in front of a classroom of

school children stood in the public gallery. This was extremely distressing. I was sent to Crown Court for trial.

The first trial date was set for early 2008. This was cancelled because the CPS had not obtained information my legal team had asked for.

The second trial date was set for Spring 2008. I had demanded to see hospital and therapy reports from the younger accuser that had been undertaken before the original accusations were levelled at me in 1999. I was told in no uncertain terms by the prosecution that I had no right to have or see such information. Unfortunately my legal team agreed. I could not believe it and decided to write to my legal team telling them that I had no confidence in their ability to defend me and asked that I be given the opportunity to seek alternative representation. In other words, I dismissed them, not realising that I would be left high and dry with no legal representation two weeks away from the trial date. I was told by my solicitor at the time that the Judge was not prepared to move the trial date. Panic set in.

With the help of the BFMS and a close friend who had been through a similar situation I eventually found a solicitor who was sympathetic to my desperate plight. I was advised to write to the court to explain why I had taken the actions I did.

Fortunately the court accepted my reasons for dismissing my previous legal team and with the help of my new legal team I was granted a new trial date for the autumn of 2008.

I am convinced if I had attended any of the two previous trial dates I would have gone to prison. The reason I say that is that with the additional time allowed both my wife and I unearthed evidence that was to be proved critical to my defence.

My wife and I worked very hard with my new legal team. A witness statement was acquired from the other sister-in-law who was supporting me and because I was of good character and had never been on the wrong side of the law, I acquired very good character references from a number of people.

Between my wife, solicitor and barrister we managed to get prepared for the pending trial. I was extremely nervous. My barrister told me it was 50/50, especially with it being of an historical nature.

The trial started promptly with the first day being taken up by swearing in the jury and the summing up of the eight indictments by the prosecution which were all subsequently proved to be absolutely false.

After lunch on the first day one of the complainants gave evidence. This was carried out first of all by showing a DVD to the court and jury. After the DVD had been seen, the older sister-in-law came into court to give her evidence hidden behind a curtain. She was asked by my barrister why she had in the past moved a hundred miles down the country to live near us, allowed her children to be babysat by my wife and me, why she allowed her daughter to stay overnight at our house on at least three occasions, why she visited our house on a regular basis, why she went on holidays as a couple and as a family with my wife and me, sent me loving birthday cards from all their family including her children, why she asked me for a job in a department that I managed and then was asked the ultimate question by my barrister why would she do this if I was the 'monster' she made me out to be. She stuttered and could not give a rational reason why. Obviously her malicious, destructive lies had caught up with her.

On the second day it was the turn of the other complainant. She also was asked by my barrister why she had accused me of the alleged abuse when my wife and I had helped her more than any other member of the family, especially when she was suffering from anorexia. She even lived with us on at least three occasions for months on end. 'Why would you want to stay at the alleged abuser's house?' she was asked.

She was then asked, if the alleged abuse happened, then why didn't she tell anyone? Her excuse was that she did not want to cause trouble in the family. My barrister then reminded her that if she had told the doctors or therapists of the alleged abuse then they (the practitioners) would not have been allowed to tell anyone without her permission, and the fact is that nothing appeared on the reports. She had no comment or excuse to offer.

The third day was taken up by my defence. I, along with my wife and the other, non-accusing sister, stood there and told the jury without hesitation the absolute truth, after which the prosecution along with my defence gave a summary of the respective evidence arguments.

On the fourth and final day of the trial the judge gave her summary to the jury. I thought it was still very much 50/50 the way the verdict would fall.

The jury were sent out around 12.20 p.m. to decide. Within half-an-hour I was called back into court. The jury needed to hear again one of the prosecution witness statements. Then the jury went back to deliberate.

The court adjourned for lunch but at two minutes past 2 p.m. I was asked to attend court. My barrister told me that a verdict had been agreed. I thought the worst.

The jury came back into court. I was flanked by two guards. My wife, son and close friends were in the public gallery. The jury foreman was asked by the judge if they had all agreed a verdict. She said yes; it was a unanimous verdict.

The court official read out the indictments one at a time. On each and every one of the charges I was found Not Guilty. The result was greeted by cries of sheer relief from my wife, son and friends; even though they had known I was not guilty.

After the final verdict of not guilty, the Judge asked the guards to release me. The judge also added that she concurred with the jury's verdict.

The relief inside me was overwhelming. I hugged and cried with my wife, son and close friends.

The situation I found myself in could happen to anyone, no matter who they are or what they are. I would not wish it on my worst enemy.

I thank Madeline Greenhalgh and Donna of the BFMS, my direct family, my sister-in-law and her husband, my close friends, one of whom stayed at my wife's side throughout the trial, and obviously my solicitor and barrister.

16. An open letter to parents (2005 to 2008)

This is the experience of one couple related by the wife of the consequences of their daughters' counselling. It is in the form of an open letter to other parents.

I am writing this in the hope that all of you, who are going through the dreadful legal system of defending yourselves against horrendous false allegations, will get courage from our experience.

My husband T was arrested in August 2005 on suspicion of rape, two months later he was charged with eight counts of rape and seven counts of lesser sexual offences. My world fell apart; I was devastated, in total shock and felt like a steam train going aimlessly along a track. I wanted the court case to be heard tomorrow so that I could put things right. For that fleeting second I gave my daughters the benefit of the doubt but common sense prevailed.

I know every case is different, but with us, my two daughters had been abused by my previous husband when they were very young. They have been receiving counselling on and off for over twenty years. But my biggest shock was my third daughter who, very much a mummy's girl, started counselling in 2004 for an eating disorder, and was now contributing to her sisters' allegations.

In the beginning, T told me that had I not stood by him, he would not have found the strength to fight believing that he had no chance of defending himself against something like this. We were very grateful that my son, in his mid twenties, stood by us.

I was not computer literate when all this started, and was writing every thing out in long hand, and presented our legal team with over a thousand pages of emotional diarrhoea, but much needed information. Then in January 2006, my son showed me how to use the Internet. At first, I was typing in 'liars,' 'untrue accusations,' and then by chance, 'false memory,' and behold, I came across the BFMS. I was in tears when I first rang Madeline, for suddenly here was a valid explanation for all the chaos that had been imposed upon us. In a way, it increased my anxiety as I was now questioning why the police and the Crown Prosecution Service had not explored this avenue before pressing charges. I now realise, that this is how the system works.

T's first trial was in February 2007. The very thought of what we were about to go through absolutely terrified us. It began to take its toll on our health. I left my hospital bed to give evidence, against the advice of the Doctors, and was not strong enough to deal with the prosecution's bombardment of questions. The whole trial was a complicated mess and it finished with a hung jury. I remember weeping when I heard the judge setting a new trial date and thinking I can't go through all this again. The new date was for September 2007. I spent most of the summer in and out of hospital, blighted with asthma which of course is brought on by stress; it was a vicious circle. Then on 2nd September, T suffered a transient ischaemic attack (a minor stroke which is a warning of a major one). I remember thinking how much more is 'He' up there, going to throw at us.

T was in hospital for over two weeks and was deemed not fit for the trial and a new date was set for 3rd January 2008, our legal team at this point were convinced that T would be found guilty at the next trial; they almost gave up on us, and we were told that a new point of law meant the jury would not be told of the eleven other men that my daughters have accused of rape. Thankfully, Madeline emailed some very important facts for our team, who in turn, found a different way of presenting our case. I had also stumbled across a family video, filmed in 2003, showing my daughters behaving quite normally around T.

It was decided that I would not give evidence at this trial, as it became obvious that the prosecution were going to take pot shots at me, which in turn would confuse the jury. It was a good decision, we had some very convincing witnesses and Dr Boakes was most compelling as our expert witness. The jury deliberated for three days. As T left for Court, I was convinced he would not come home that night. His last words to me were 'sell the house, get what you can for it, and make a new life for yourself.' I was at rock bottom. I weighed six and a half stone and felt as if I were going to have a stroke. At 12.30 p.m. I received the first call from T, the jury were still deliberating, but had found him not guilty on all the rape charges. I almost collapsed, and rang Madeline in tears to let her know, and I remember her saying 'enjoy the moment.' At 4 p.m. T called to say it was all over and he was on his way home. It was a very emotional evening.

I am writing this exactly one week later. Coping without all the stress is very strange. I am still doing battle in my dreams, but we now have the rest of our lives together. My anger is not with my daughters, but with the system, and the sadness that I have lost them and our six grand children. When I have recovered my strength, I intend to start fighting back at this hideous system and the witch hunt tactics of the police. They never came to me during their investigation. And, as for the detective constable involved in the case, I do hope that when he returns to his family at the end of his working day, he feels very proud of his achievements. Yet another fractured family.

Thank goodness for Madeline and her team. Without their interest in our case, I think I might have lost the plot. I also want to say a very big thank you to Sheila who often phoned and emailed me and gave me the strength to keep going.

17. Hope for posthumous justice (1997 to 2008)

The following case dates back to the early days of recovered memory therapy when there was even less understanding of false memories than there is now. As a result, the accused, George Davison (his real name), received one of the longest sentences ever to be imposed on the basis of allegations arising from therapy. After his release from prison, the Criminal Cases Review Commission (CCRC) agreed to review his case. Although George died before the case came to court, the CCRC has decided to continue with the review.

The following obituary, written by a friend, and published in the BFMS Newsletter March 2008 tells George's story.

George Davison (1940–2008), who died recently following an unsuccessful heart by-pass operation, was one of 17 children from a south London family who became a fighter throughout his life, not just for himself but for others. He left London to work for an engineering company and, as he gradually built up his understanding of engineering and people, he succeeded in setting up and running a successful engineering business where honesty and straight-talking got him a long way. He diversified into managing an old people's home before be decided to sell up and retire in his fifties.

Sadly his planned retirement was interrupted when he was a victim of false allegations from a patient receiving treatment at a psychiatric clinic. The situation escalated and, as this was in the early days of false memory syndrome, most people, including his barrister, did not believe him and he ended up with one of the longest sentences in a false memories case.

While in prison George's honesty and straight-talking gained him the respect of many prison officers and in at least two prisons he was given top jobs only open to the most trusted prisoners. His honesty and straight-talking didn't always endear him to all his fellow prisoners though many respected him for it and he was also able to offer a sympathetic ear which a number appreciated. He was not afraid to complain when he know things were wrong, as when he complained about a prison officer who was sexually molesting vulnerable prisoners, but this sometimes meant he ended up in the punishment block.

George kept himself physically fit in the gym and mentally fit behind his door where his cell was always neat and tidy, Radio 4 was on and he would write a steam of letters, among them those to his beloved Maggie or to yet another solicitor in the hope of getting someone to take up his case.

Following his release he spent nine pointless months in a hostel before he was allowed to go home which, as he admitted, wasn't quite as he had expected. Maggie had had to do lots of things round the house that he used to do before he went to prison and he had to get used to the fact that she could and would continue to do some of these things.

He kept up his gym and was somewhat disappointed when the doctors said that he wouldn't be able to do press-ups for three months after his operation. Six of his friends from the gym acted as pall-bearers, carrying his coffin at his funeral.

The best news came at Easter 2007 when he heard that the Criminal Case Review Commission (CCRC) had agreed to review his case; unfortunately, he did not last long enough on earth to learn the result. Though George was not an adherent of a particular religion, he did believe in God and that he could pray to him and his funeral service recognised his faith in ways I think he would have appreciated.

18. 81 Year Old Edward Swan (2007)

This case, reported by a solicitor, a member of the accuser's family but not his legal representative, is included in full in chapter 12. It is placed there because of the Solicitor's detailed analysis of the way that uncorroborated allegations made by an adult undergoing therapy are handled by the legal system. It is, however, equally relevant to this section.

It also demonstrates the fact that both men and women are susceptible to the influence of recovered memory theories and practices — the complainant in this case was male. Some ten percent of the cases on the files of the BFMS involve allegations of childhood abuse arising from 'recovered memories' made by an adult male while undergoing therapy.

Another notable aspect of this case is the assumption by the psychotherapist, readily accepted by the police and CPS, that the complainant's mental condition was a direct result of childhood abuse.

> Brown blamed his mental illness — Obsessive Compulsive Disorder (OCD) — on the 'childhood sexual abuse he had suffered'.
> The CPS was seeking to introduce this as evidence.

At a case discussion meeting attended by the complainant, the investigating policeman and the psychotherapist in February 2007, the question was posed,

> Is there an expert who can say with certainty that OCD arose out of child abuse?

19. Phillip Coates: successful appeal against Court Martial conviction for rape (2007)

All paragraph numbers refer to extracts from the transcription of the Court of Appeal's judgment 2007 EWCA Crim 1471, case number 200701598c5, available on www.bailii.org

This case demonstrates the effect of a form of treatment originating in America in the 1980s known as EMDR (Eye Movement Desensitisation and Reprocessing)[1] which played a critical part in the Court Martial's decision.

The Court-Martial had to consider four statements made by the complainant. These statements were summarised in paragraph 27 of the Appeal Court's judgment, as follows:

> The problem with these four statements does not require any substantial analysis. In the first statement made on the night in question, the essential allegation is that after kissing for a while the couple had intercourse on the sick bay bed because in the end she gave up trying to say 'no.' The second and third statements suggest the absence of any memory of the circumstances in which intercourse took place. The fourth statement conveys that intercourse took place notwithstanding the complainant's continuous struggling. Both the first and fourth statements involve allegations of rape, but there are significant differences in the circumstances in which it allegedly occurred.

It was after seeing Dr McGowan, described as an 'Accredited Consultant in (EMDR)' that the complainant made the fourth statement in which she was then able to provide a more detailed description of the alleged incident (para. 20).

The strange and disturbing feature of this case is that 'from the outset, the Crown's case was that the appellant should be convicted on the basis of the account given in the fourth statement. In fact the conviction was based on the first statement' (para. 28).

Prior to the Court-Martial, the Judge Advocate General had to consider whether the fourth statement following the complainant's visit to Dr

McGowan should be excluded. He heard evidence from Dr McGowan and Dr Dodgson, a practitioner of EMDR, for the prosecution and, for the defence, from Dr Boakes, a clinical psychiatrist and psychotherapist, a Fellow of the Royal College of Psychiatrists, (see chapter 11 and Brandon et al. [1998]). Later, after the Court-Martial commenced, Dr Mason, a clinical psychiatrist was called before the Board. The Judge Advocate General clearly had reservations about the fourth statement. But he was faced with the dilemma, following on from the prosecution's decision to base the case on the fourth statement, that if this was inadmissible 'then the whole evidence must go. It all stays or it all goes' (para. 30).

The Judge Advocate General's response to the fourth statement should have been unequivocal.

> Nevertheless he concluded that notwithstanding that the process undertaken by Dr McGowan had facilitated what was described as prememory recall in inappropriate circumstances, evidence based on the fourth statement should be admitted (para. 30).

Thus he felt able to allow the Court-Martial to go ahead.

In the event the defendant was convicted of rape and jailed for five years on the basis of an account in the first statement which was, in the words of the appeal judgment, 'an account of the incident which the complainant herself disavowed in her evidence and which did not represent the Crown's case against him. This is highly unusual' (para. 38). Having allowed the fourth statement to be admitted, presumably so the case could proceed 'on the basis of the account given in the fourth statement' (para. 28), for the Crown then to proceed on the basis of the first statement (para. 38) was not just 'highly unusual,' to the lay observer it appears perverse.

Several comments made in the Appeal Court judgment provide an indication of the Judge Advocate General's uncertainty when faced with evidence arising from therapy:

i. In his ruling the Judge Advocate General concluded that it was agreed between the experts that the memories described in the fourth statement could be fact or fiction ... he was persuaded that the fourth statement was unreliable ... however he did not exclude it, nor indicate that he would direct the Board to ignore it (para. 34).

ii. He (the Judge Advocate General) said that the fairness of the trial could be guaranteed by very careful directions, with particular emphasis on difficulties arising from the involvement of Dr McGowan with the complainant (para. 35).

But see the Appeal Court's comments in v. below regarding the quality of these directions.

iii. The Judge Advocate General directed the Board to 'exercise caution before they acted on the unsupported memories of the complainant after the therapeutic session with Dr McGowan'. However he left open the possibility of a conviction for rape on that basis. He summarised the evidence of the experts in detail. He did not comment on the reliability, or otherwise, of the fourth statement, or the evidence based on it, or the consequences of the complainant's therapy with Dr McGowan (para. 37).

iv. The Board had to consider whether to convict the appellant either on the basis of the complainant's testimony or on the basis of her first statement.

This required a careful analysis of the potential difficulties to the defence generated by what we shall describe as the McGowan process, and the deficiencies and unreliability of the evidence consequent upon it. We need not spend any time on this aspect of the case because, as we know, the Board rejected the post McGowan evidence. The Judge Advocate General, however, was also required to give extremely careful directions about the approach of the Board to the evidence, if they found, as they did, that the post McGowan evidence was unreliable (para. 44).

v. Without laying down any formalised straitjacket for the directions which the Board should have been given, the directions which were given were not as full or complete as, in the very unusual circumstances of this case, they required to be (para. 44).

vi. In our judgment, this conviction is unsafe, and must be quashed (para. 45).

20. Malcolm's story: institutional prejudice within the legal system against the concept of false memory? (1998 to 2007)

The facts

This case-history is unusual, if not unique, in that notes of a psychologist's interview with a family member were used in defence of the accused in two separate court cases.

The comments in the Crown Court Pre-Trial judgment (at the second court case) give particular cause for concern. Why were the social services, police and CPS blind to the overwhelming evidence of contradictions, inconsistencies and undue influence so obvious to the Crown Court Judge (and to the magistrate in the first case)? Was this because of ignorance of the dangers of accepting as evidence allegations based on memories 'recovered' during therapy? Or was there an immovable prejudice against the concept of false memory, as described by Katharine Mair in chapter 6.

Allegations were made against Malcolm firstly by his daughter and, seven years later, by his granddaughter, both of whom were living with his ex-wife. In both cases the allegations were rejected by the courts and he was found Not Guilty. A feature of both was the influence on mother and daughter of the discredited self-help book, *The courage to heal* [Bass and Davis, 1988].

In the first court case historical allegations of childhood abuse were made by the 32 year old daughter against her father, Malcolm. They arose after she was referred by social services to a hypnotherapist and stage-hypnotist. During this therapy, the daughter claimed to have recovered memories of sexual abuse dating back to the age of six. The case was thrown out at the preliminary hearing at the magistrates' court because of inconsistencies in the evidence provided by the defendant's ex-wife, the social services, the police and the CPS.

At the time these allegations were made, the granddaughter was interviewed by a psychologist and repeatedly denied having been abused by him. The psychologist's notes were used as defence evidence in the later court case against Malcolm, as described below.

Unfortunately, as in so many cases, at the time of his arrest, the police gave Malcolm's name to the press and this was published with a photograph. No publicity was given to the decisions of both the Magistrates' and (later) the Crown Court to return Not Guilty verdicts.

The second court case arose seven years later when the granddaughter, then aged fourteen, and under the supervision of social services was referred to a mental health team by her family doctor. Her behaviour had deteriorated following her mother's marriage and the arrival of a new family, and she became severely depressed. Records of interviews with the daughter during this time show that in response to repeated questioning about her relationship with her grandfather she had given the same answer each time, 'He never touched me. I love my grandfather.' It was only at the end of this lengthy process that she came to believe that her problems were caused by having been sexually abused by him at the age of six, events which she claimed she had until then totally forgotten.

The Crown Court judge stopped the case at the pre-trial hearing and returned a verdict of 'Not Guilty,' with costs awarded to the defendant. The reasons given by the judge included:

> contamination of this girl's evidence, living in the household she did, and the animosity towards the defendant which undoubtedly there was. But in general terms she lived within a very dysfunctional family from everyone's point of view and this is confirmed by the information now disclosed by Social Services records that the argument for contamination is extremely strong. And on the basis that burden of proof rests with the prosecution to exclude the possibility that this is the result of contamination within the household of the girl's family, I just do not see how the Prosecution can even start to discharge that burden and in those circumstances, I think it would be wholly unfair for the evidence to be called ... I can see no part at all for a judge to allow a case to start and go on to the end of the Prosecution case in the knowledge that he is going to stop the case. It seems to be an abuse in the situation to do that. It is not fair to go to a jury in those circumstances.

The notes of the psychologist's interviews with the granddaughter at the time of the first court case provided crucial evidence in the second court case. She had repeatedly denied that she had been abused by her grandfather.

A commentary on how prejudiced the jury system is against those who are faced with historical allegations of child abuse was provided by the Crown Court Judge who, following his judgment, told Malcolm that despite the weight of evidence for the defence, he would probably have been found guilty by a jury. The judge, presumably, was aware of the powerful emotional impact on juries of false (recovered) memories in which complainants describe fictional ordeals in considerable and colourful detail. Without clear direction from the judiciary on the unreliability of memories allegedly recovered in therapy, there is a very real danger of a miscarriage of justice — as demonstrated in other cases featured in this section where guilty verdicts returned by juries were overturned on appeal.

An emotional roller-coaster

Before the experiences described above, Malcolm was a respected member of the community with a wide circle of friends and godparent to a number of their children. In his own words, 'I worshipped my granddaughter.' Their relationship was one of love and friendship and he would have willingly given his life to protect her — as was confirmed by the testimony of friends and neighbours. The Crown Court judge described him as 'very open and honest' and commented that he hoped 'this horrific process was now at an end for you.'

The events that followed a very acrimonious divorce marked the point when Malcolm's life was to change for ever when he was accused of abuse against his daughter who was living with her mother — Malcolm's ex-wife. This time, through to early 1999, he described as 'very traumatic' but he had no idea then what was to come. He is unable to find words to describe this experience, 'like being emotionally turned inside out, and then turned inside out again, then again.'

Malcolm is now living alone, without contact with his family and friends. His experience, as with virtually every case involving allegations based on 'recovered' memories (whether or not legal action followed), demonstrates that the damage they cause never fully heals.

21. *R* v *X*: successful appeal against convictions for indecent assault and rape (2000 to 2006)

Reporting of the case of *R* v *X* is heavily circumscribed by legal constraints. However, '*X*' was able to provide the following comment:

> an alarming aspect of this case is the refusal of the Crown Prosecution Service to listen to the opinion of their own expert witness, a psychiatrist who, among other things, works at a prison dealing with sex offenders, and then to the clearly expressed view of their second expert witness. Even though the Criminal Cases Review Commission's report and the evidence of the expert witness commissioned by the CCRC had clearly indicated that their line of attack on the defence at the original trial had been utterly wrong, they insisted on pursuing the case at the Court of Appeal and at re-trial until it became clear that all the evidence they were turning up supported the innocence of the defendant. They conceded with very bad grace and the defendant was formally acquitted at the re-trial.

R v *X* reached the Appeal Court for the second time in June 2005, four and a half years after *X* had received a twelve-year jail sentence for alleged offences of indecent assault and rape.

The appeal

The following report of the appeal by the ICLR (Incorporated Council of Law Reporting) contains references to the unreliability of evidence based on the period of 'childhood amnesia' that should have sounded a note of caution to judges hearing cases where all or part of the evidence is based on 'memories' allegedly recovered by a complainant in therapy.

R v *X* (Childhood Amnesia) CA: Smith L J, Hughes and Wakerley J J: 1 July 2005

Expert evidence as to a phenomenon known as 'childhood amnesia' was admissible as likely to be outside the knowledge and experience of a judge or jury.

The Court of Appeal, Criminal Division, so held in allowing an appeal by *X*, on a reference by the Criminal Cases Review Commission against his conviction on four counts of rape and two counts of indecent assault.

SMITH LJ, giving the judgment of the court, said that the victim of the offences claimed to have memories going back to before she was three years old. In her witness statement, made at the age of 19, she had given very detailed narrative accounts, in relation to the offences of rape, of three specific incidents of sexual intercourse. At the hearing of the appeal the defence were given leave to call fresh evidence, *de bene esse*, from a professor of cognitive psychology who had worked for about 25 years on memory formation and autobiographical memory. The professor gave evidence that the memories of a child were qualitatively different from the memories of later events. The period of 'childhood amnesia' usually extended up to the age of seven and he had never come across a person who had been able to provide a detailed account of something that had happened to them at the age of four or five. His explanation was that during the first five years of life the frontal lobes of the brain were in a state of rapid change and development. He said that a detailed narrative account of an event during those years of childhood should be treated with caution, especially if it contained a number of details which were extraneous points. The court came to the conclusion that the evidence was true expert evidence suitable for admission at a trial and it would only be in the most unusual circumstances, such as the present, that such evidence would be relevant. The appeal would be allowed, the conviction quashed and a re-trial ordered.

Reported by Clare Barsby, barrister

22. *R v Bowman*: unsuccessful appeal against conviction in 2002 for the murder of his wife: *R v Bowman* [2006] EWCA Crim 417 (2 March 2006)

It appears, from the determination, that the judges, defence and prosecution counsel involved in the appeal struggled to understand memory in general and, in particular, the distinction between 'always remembered' childhood memories and memories allegedly completely forgotten and 'remembered' many years later in adulthood while undergoing therapy.

NOTE: this is a complex case and needs to be viewed in two parts: the claim made by Thomas Bowman's daughter, that, while in therapy, twenty years after the alleged event, she recovered memories in considerable detail of her father murdering her mother; and the subsequent, widely divergent and conflicting opinions on the *post mortem* evidence provided by eight expert witness pathologists and forensic scientists at the time of death, at the trial and at the appeal.

Mr Bowman's conviction dates back to when his daughter, Diane, claimed that, while undergoing therapy and having read the self-help book, *The courage to heal*, she 'remembered' him murdering his wife 22 years earlier. She reported this to the police, the body was exhumed and a second autopsy was carried out by Dr Armour, a Home Office pathologist. She concluded that death was due to manual strangulation. In 2002 Mr Bowman was convicted of murder and sentenced to life imprisonment. It was the safety of this autopsy evidence that primarily figured in the appeal judgment.

The following is a selection of key paragraphs from the lengthy appeal court judgment that relates to the safety of evidence based on memories arising during therapy (A longer summary of the judgment can be found in Burgoyne [2006]. The full judgment can be obtained on www.bailii.org).

Mr Bowman lost his appeal.

Appeal extracts

The prosecution evidence at the trial

> relied upon a number of strands of evidence in support of its case on the count of murder (transcript of the Appeal Court determination, para. 6).

> The principal evidence relied upon by the prosecution was evidence of what happened on the night of 7/8 July 1978; and evidence from forensic scientists ... the prosecution also called a Kevin Williams, a prisoner serving a sentence in the same prison where the appellant was in custody awaiting trial.

The prosecution called upon evidence from members of the family (paras 6 and 7) concerning the alleged violent behaviour of the appellant towards members of his family.

Damien and Diane, the appellant's son and daughter, gave evidence alleging sexual abuse.

> Her evidence was that sexual abuse by the appellant on her began when she was about 5 years old. Count 2 was an allegation of indecent assault which took place between 1 January 1978 and 9 July 1978 (para. 8).

In paragraphs 8 to 10 Diane and Damien (he was eight at the time) gave a detailed description of events on the day before and the night their mother died.

The coroner instituted an investigation and an autopsy was carried out that concluded that death was caused by alcohol and Valium poisoning (paras 12 and 13).

> *In 1995 Diane moved to Northern Ireland. In 1998 she made a statement that she had never been sexually abused by the appellant. In evidence she said that she believed that at the time she made the statement because she had suppressed the memories of what had happened. In late 1998 she started having counselling and began to remember incidents. As a result of her memory recall she contacted the police in 2000.* As a result of what she told the police the body of the deceased was exhumed on 21 March 2001. Dr Armour (a forensic pathologist) was present at the exhumation and carried out the autopsy shortly afterwards (para. 15).

> On the basis of these (Dr Armour's) findings, she concluded that death was caused by manual strangulation. She asserted that

there was no other explanation for the death of the deceased (para. 16).

Paragraphs 17 to 19 dealt with the reliability of the original autopsy report, a toxicology report at the time of death and Dr Armour's later report.

The fellow prisoner gave evidence of conversations he said he had had with the appellant (paras 21 and 22).

Paragraphs 23 to 27 were concerned with the evidence given by the appellant, supporting testimony from members of his family and the reliability of the original autopsy and toxicology reports. The defence also produced another prisoner who gave evidence.

> He said that he had shared a cell with Williams (the first prisoner). He said that Williams had formed the opinion that the appellant was guilty and was determined to make him admit it. He even spoke of 'stitching him up.'

Of the seven grounds put forward for the appeal, only one ground was allowed (paras 28 to 29). This involved considering lengthy and complex expert witness evidence from five pathologists. There were strong differences of opinion between not only the defence and prosecution expert witnesses, but also between those called by the prosecution counsel (paras 69 to 159). The Appeal Court was sufficiently concerned at the presentation of expert witness evidence that at the end of its decision it offered its own 'necessary inclusions' on their use, as a rider to the instructions given by the Attorney General (paras 174 to 178).

Paragraphs 30 and 31 were concerned with reliability of the evidence recalled by the daughter during therapy. Paragraph 30 states,

> We need to refer to only two other grounds. They were grounds 3 and 5. Ground 3 alleged a failure by the defence team to seek expert advice in relation to the inherent incapacity of a 5 year old to retain complex facts, emotions and reasoning and a failure to elicit the precise state of the medical records in so far as they bore on the evidence of the children. Linked with this ground was ground 5 which alleged that Dr Boakes, an expert on the cognitive ranges of memory of young children and available to the defence ought to have been called. The Court refused leave on both grounds on the basis that Dr Boakes was available to give evidence on behalf of the defence and the decision not to call her was not one which could be characterised as Wednesbury unreasonable[1] (para. 31).

> Mr David Martin-Sperry, counsel for the appellant, but not trial counsel, does not now criticise the defence for not calling Dr

Boakes. He seeks leave to substitute two further grounds for appeal. We shall refer to them as grounds 2 and 3. Ground 2 is that there is fresh evidence from Professor Conway, an expert in memory research, which it is contended is such as, if received, would throw doubt on the evidence of Diane. Ground 3 invites the Court to rule as unsafe the verdicts of guilty on the remaining counts on the indictment in the event that the Court allows the appeal against conviction on count 1.

Following consideration of expert witness evidence on the reliability of the pathology reports, Lord Carlile (leading counsel for the defence) gave the following reasons for not calling Dr Boakes to give evidence at the trial:

Lord Carlile was asked about his decision not to call Dr Boakes. He said that in cross-examination of Diane he had elicited sufficient to enable him to construct an argument that her claimed recollection of what had occurred at the time of her mother's death was 'recovered memory.' Until this cross-examination there was no evidence to justify Diane's evidence in this way. He said that although the suggestion that Diane's evidence was recovered memory was available he had real doubts that this was so. The reality was more probably that the counselling she had undergone had reawakened horrible memories in a mechanism very different from recovered memory techniques. Nevertheless, as soon as the issue arose, he advised that Dr Janet Boakes should be consulted as a matter of urgency. She produced a report that was served on the prosecution. The prosecution in turn served a report from Professor Brewin that expressed the view that Diane's recollection was not recovered memory and stated that Diane's memory processes were acceptable and explicable in conventional terms (para. 67).

In the event it was decided not to call Dr Boakes because it was thought that she would be liable to successful cross-examination by the prosecution in which event her views could not be used in the closing speech. Lord Carlile was also concerned that if he called Dr Boakes, the way would be open to the prosecution to adduce the appellant's conviction in 1998 for the rape of ... (a previous conviction for sexual offences against his step daughter) (para. 68).

The Court agreed to hear the evidence from Professor Conway '*de bene esse*' (that is, well done for the present, but conditionally heard without making a decision on whether to repeat it) (paras 160 to 169).

His (Professor Conway's) written report set out general comments about the unreliability of memories of children at a distance of 20 years remove or more. In general terms the report pointed to the difficulties of accurately recalling events occurring at age 5 when re-telling them after 20 or more years. In the summary of paragraph 2 of his report Professor Conway stated:

> *2.5 Summary. The memories from below about 7 years in age were formed during the period in which the brain, the self, memory comprehension, language, and the emotions were all undergoing rapid and intense development. Memories from this time are likely to contain errors and in some cases will be entirely wrong. This is the case for everyone, there is nothing unusual about it and it simply reflects the fact that, in humans more so than in any other animal, cognition develops after birth. It means, however, that memories from this period, when the individual was aged 5 to 7 years or less should be treated with caution. As a memory researcher I would not rely on the accuracy of such memories unless there was additional, independent, corroborating evidence* (para. 161).

The Appeal Court summarised Professor Conway's oral evidence:

> He said that it was not impossible for a child of 5½ to remember her mother being murdered. He added most people remember three or four 'hot spots' in their early life. However he said research shows that the memory of early events is recalled out of order and with inaccuracies as to the detail of the event or events. In his opinion the only way to test the accuracy of such evidence is by looking at independent reliable evidence which supports it. He said that in his opinion it was not possible for an adult to relate accurately conversations heard under the age of seven (para. 162).

> Generally he (Professor Conway) was sceptical about false memory syndrome. He said it was a hypothesis for which there was no proper evidence. He was asked in cross examination if much of what he was saying was simple common sense. He said he did not really know (para. 163).

NOTE: this opinion by Professor Conway that 'he really did not know' if much of what he was saying was simple common sense, is not consistent with the Court's later interpretation of his opinion :

> Essentially, the professor's evidence of the results of the research into memories goes little further than is commonsense and well within normal human experience (para. 168).

In the same paragraph, the Court adds:

> He (Professor Conway) accepted that a traumatic event occurring when a person is under the age of seven can be recalled by that person in adulthood. Moreover, rejecting, as he does, false memory syndrome, it would not have assisted Lord Carlile's attempts in cross-examination to sow the seeds of that hypothesis in the minds of the jury (para. 168).

NOTE: the Court also appears to have ignored Professor Conway's opinion that it was not possible for an adult to relate accurately conversations heard under the age of seven.

Further debate on the reasons for not calling Dr Boakes as an expert witness for the appellant followed (paras 166 and 167) with the apparent recognition by the Court that there remained doubt over this issue:

> Whether the reason for not calling Dr Boakes was right or wrong, having heard Professor Conway's evidence we are quite satisfied that his evidence would not have assisted the appellant if it had been given at the trial. In our judgment it is on the very borderline of admissibility (para. 168).

Finally the Court stated,

> Generally the contradictions in Diane's evidence and her failure to give a version of the killing which accorded with strangulation (the prosecution contended that her view of what happened at the crucial time was hidden by the appellant's body) were all before the jury. The judge directed the jury to take great care in assessing her evidence. We are quite satisfied that if Professor Conway's evidence had been given at the trial it would not have affected the verdicts and it affords no ground for allowing the appeal. In the circumstances we reject the application for leave to amend the grounds for appeal in the terms sought (para. 169).

23. 'E': trial judge orders charges to be dropped after defendant's two years of hell because of false memories

E's views on the legal system's handling of his case are given in chapter 13.

At a Crown Court hearing all charges against Mr E were dropped on the order of the judge. They were:

- two counts of rape and

- seven counts of indecent assault and gross indecency.

The charges were first laid against Mr E, a respected citizen and public servant, after he was arrested at his home.

He spent thousands of pounds in research and legal fees to clear his name. He and his family, friends and colleagues and fellow voluntary workers had to live for two years with the public knowledge that these allegations had been made.

The charges arose after the intervention in the lives of the accusers — a daughter and a step daughter whom he had adopted at a very early age — by various psychiatric and social services agencies. They resulted from instances of 'recovered memory.'

The period involved stretched back, as the dates of the charges indicate, over 40 years.

Two years on Mr E still awaits the decision of the court on how much he will be awarded in costs.

During the course of the police enquiries a detective told a third daughter of Mr E who did not support the allegations or have any to make herself, 'If you cannot add to my case I don't need to speak to you.' The daughter challenged the officer over this and was told dismissively, 'You have been abused but won't admit it.'

Describing the end of his ordeal before criminal law, Mr E said:

> When the charges against me were dropped my solicitor rang
> to inform me and I then had to appear at the Crown Court for

the formal legal request to the Judge for a formal finding of Not Guilty.

I had been originally due to appear before the judge who had been the trial judge in the case from early days and who had been quite critical of both the CPS and the police during the proceedings. However, two days before that hearing I was contacted late in the afternoon by our solicitor who told me my case had been transferred to another Crown Court. This was because the CPS barrister had business there that day.

The consequence of this was that the judge now appointed knew nothing of the case and so there was a run through of the headline allegations before the reasons were given for asking for the Not Guilty verdict. None of the lurid allegations were left out.

The barrister explained that 'due to inconsistencies and contra-dictions' of the complainants and the obvious great distance in time since the alleged events, there was now no prospect of se-curing a conviction. Therefore the decision had been taken to discontinue the case against me.

The last minute change of venue and the recapitulation of the prosecution case was no doubt procedurally necessary but it was a gratuitous twist of the knife in my wound.

However, my barrister, welcoming the decision to drop the case, was again able to put the other side by saying that from the very beginning the prosecution case was a very weak one. He mentioned the inadequate investigations, lack of records and my good character; also that from the very beginning I had vigor-ously denied the charges.

My barrister also asked for a contribution to our costs as we had been put to a great expense researching the reasons for the allegations, photography, printing, travel and telephones as we had literally trawled the world looking for ex neighbours, school friends and ex boy-friends. 'My client has carried out, at his own expense, an immense amount of work that would ordinarily have to be done and paid for at considerably greater cost. The work he, his wife and daughter, and his friends have carried out has saved the public purse many thousands of pounds', explained the barrister.

A message from the non-accusing daughter of Mr E

My dad, whose story is told above, has been triumphantly vindicated, thanks to years of hard work and research and the support he has received throughout from a close circle of friends, colleagues and advisers and above all my mum.

The Crown Court judge threw out a ramp of terrifying charges against my dad without any evidence being heard. I was so glad for that but this has been no simple 'happy ending.'

Just at the time of the first accusation there were stories repeatedly emerging into the public domain, that when troubled people looked into their past, sexual abuse might be discerned as the cause — regardless of the facts. Unfortunately this was when things blew up for my dad. At first I felt under pressure to join in the allegations but there was not the tiniest shadow of a thought in my whole experience of my dad that could make me doubt him.

He is, in his quiet way, a respected public figure in the town and perhaps because of his position the police saw my father as something of a special target. What I felt was their disdainful treatment of him and indifference to me, indeed a reluctance to listen to me and my defence of my father, pointed to that.

One of them told me: 'If you cannot add to my case, I don't need to speak to you.' I was even accused of being 'in denial.' I was incredibly angry.

When I first heard the allegations I was living abroad. My whole being switched into safety mode. As a mum with a tiny baby I didn't want to have to think about it. I put up mental barricades. I stayed still. I lost all yardsticks of normality. And when Dad said: 'I will take Freddie up for his bath,' I found myself saying: 'I will do it.'

The following morning I realised this was rubbish. It wasn't because I doubted him. It was because I doubted what was going on.

When the police became involved I didn't describe my feelings to my parents. I didn't want to add to their worries. I had to live with it. I did try to deal with it on my own, from France, where I was working. But there was a point when I had a sixth sense that there was something dreadfully wrong.

When I was first approached by my two sisters I kept things to myself. I wrote to them and said 'I don't think that I have been abused' and I thought that would be it. Then I told my parents. I had been trying to protect them. I now wish I had warned them straight away.

I think that in my elder (step) sister's case, recovered 'memory' was what drove her. I think she had a conscience. When it came to the words in her statement to the police they were just not hers. She knew in her heart that this was wrong.

How have I coped since all this blew up? It knocked me off balance at first. I developed a very short temper. At work it was noticed and commented on too. If anyone started talking about sex abuse cases I just snapped: 'You don't know what you are talking about.' People could have wondered why I was like that.

Also, I work in a children's environment. If my father had been found guilty it would have branded me a liar. Thankfully I had a lot of support from my employer whom I told on a need-to-know basis. I would not have got through otherwise.

And my own children suffered. I fell into a routine of work, cook, research. On one occasion I was so preoccupied that I found that the children had fallen asleep where they were. But I was determined to contain the pain and shock — not to pass the poison on.

I passed on information to my children in 'headline' form according to the stages of their growing up. They are 16 and 13 now and this situation was against the whole basis of how they had been brought up.

Having seen the way the police didn't want to check or investigate any information which did not back up their belief in my father's guilt, I can't trust the justice system any more.

Our family remains broken. Perhaps, by now, any hopes of our being a normal family have faded so far as to be irrelevant. To haunt us, however, there are still the photograph albums, the treasured mementos and now, the grandchildren, nieces and cousins whom we will never know. And who will not know us.

Memories are individual, personal. They are what helps you to go on. These accusations have violated my memories. People do need to understand that that these things have a fallout afterwards that can change the whole way that you continue to live your life.

24. The police lied to my wife (2004 to 2006)

This father's story was first reported in Fractured families *[Brand, 2007] and is updated here.*

Following the false accusations made against me by one of my three daughters that I had abused her between the ages of 4 and 9, I returned — with my wife, — to the UK from America where I was working as a pastor at the time. I went straight to the police and voluntarily arranged to submit myself for questioning.

On arriving at the police station I was held for about seven hours, during which time I was questioned on a number of occasions and in between kept locked in a police cell with my shoes removed. It was a horrendous experience and one I would not wish to repeat.

During the day they telephoned my wife who was waiting for me in the local area, and asked her if she would submit herself for questioning too, which she agreed to do.

The police then questioned her on the same issues they raised with me and at one point blatantly lied to her in an attempt to gain a confession, by telling her that I had 'broken down and confessed to everything' — which was absolutely not true, not least because there was nothing for me to confess to!

After being released on bail without having to pay any security bond, I was then left waiting for six months as the police decided whether they had enough evidence to present to the CPS. I was told three times within that period that the decision would be taken but each time this was delayed as they said they needed more time.

After six awful months of waiting, the police, following some considerable prompting from my solicitor, said they had decided to drop all charges against me. There were three primary reasons:

- the medical evidence did not match up

- the witness statements did not support the allegations

- they were particularly impressed with a photograph taken two years earlier with a picture of my daughter who had made the allegations sitting on my lap with her arm around me and smiling, a picture they said did not match up to the events she claimed had taken place 14 years earlier.

While we have done our best to rebuild our shattered lives there remains an overwhelming sense of injustice as our reputation has been destroyed with the people we called our friends. Nothing I have been able to do or say has connected them to the truth and they continue to treat us as though I am guilty. Not a day goes by even now after over three years that I do not rehearse everything that has happened and wonder what I could have said or done differently that would have changed the outcome and helped provide a breakthrough for our daughter.

We still hope to be reunited with our accusing daughter but every time we attempt to make contact, everything we say gets twisted and manipulated, it would seem by both her and those around her, and then thrown back at us — as though we were guilty of some great crime in trying to renew contact with her.

I am sure that in reading this you will sense the hurt and outrage we feel at all that we have been put through, however, the most hurtful and frustrating thing in all of this is that we feel powerless to help our daughter. As her parents we have sown so much into her life over the years and now see her going through something she should never have had to face, but are being kept away from her at arms length in some perverse attempt to 'protect' her. In reality all that is happening is that she is being left to try and come to terms with what she believes has happened with absolutely no hope of closure for her. She believes I am living in denial but the opposite is true and nothing we try to do seems to be able to change the situation.

We love our daughter so deeply and the fact that we are unable to express this to her is so hurtful, and to know that she must be absolutely miserable with what she believes, makes it doubly difficult to bear. Who is out there helping these victims of false memory? Who is able to look beyond the trauma they are experiencing and get to the truth? It is so difficult to see how this can ever change, and therefore so important that the False Memory Societies are supported and continue to challenge the counselling community to review its methods.

Interestingly, we are told that they have been assured by an 'expert counsellor' that there is 'absolutely no possibility she could have a false memory.' That people are naïve enough and so ill-informed to believe this astonishes me. It shows the ignorance in both the counselling community and in the general public at large, that they can dismiss such a possibility without hesitation and make such a ridiculous statement. It does not seem to have occurred to them that it is impossible to tell when someone has a false memory, and that if it were so, there would not be a False Memory Society in existence anywhere in the world as they would be totally irrelevant, and every case could be decided by an 'expert counsellor'. Utterly terrifying and blatantly not true!

Life, however, goes on and we try to remain positive and enjoy the rest of our family as best we can. However this unfinished business is left hanging over us and I sometimes wonder if it will ever be resolved, and whether reconciliation can take place before it is too late and we are gone with the truth never having been revealed.

25. Doctors, heal yourselves: 'not one scintilla of evidence' (late 1990s)

First published in Fractured families *[Brand, 2007] and updated here.*

The sad, awful thing about all this is that I have to blame fellow members of the healing professions for bringing this situation about. Jenny had been treated for an overdose, stemming in part from our family worries during a distressing marital break-up, which had worsened her situation from other routine teenage problems. It became very clear that she needed to be helped in a supportive environment. Being in the medical profession I, with the agreement of her mother, sought the opinion of a local well-respected child psychiatrist.

What began with the damaging effect on my daughter of her parents' marital break-up, led to my being charged and remanded to a Crown Court, accused of having sexually abused her. This was after nine months of police investigation.

I have recounted what happened next in *Fractured families*. As I wrote there:

> I did not realise at the time but this was, by a long, long way, the worst mistake that I have ever made. It led her, [my daughter] by way of a spurious threat to be sectioned under mental health legislation, to a child and adolescent psychiatric unit, although at the time I felt a sense of overwhelming relief that she was safely in the hands of professionals.

> In this unit, and over many months, she was given no option other than to become estranged from her family (part of the 'therapy' I was subsequently informed). Additionally she had enforced loss of contact with all her friends. She received no educational input, was inappropriately subjected to a variety of since discredited psychotropic drugs, even though she had no mental illness, and exposed to repeated and protracted biased group therapy ('Tell me what you want and I'll believe you' — Community Psychiatric Nurse).

We had acted, as we thought, for the best, but in referring our daughter to the 'professionals' we unwittingly put her at the mercy of a culture which actively encouraged young people to make anti-parental judgments, especially against fathers. In my case this led my daughter's psychiatric advisors to encourage her to accuse a teacher, an old family friend and finally her father of having sexually abused her. Charges were not pursued against anyone but me however. Do I have to say, even now and after the judge totally exonerated me that I did nothing of the sort? The answer to that will, sadly, always be 'Yes.'

The judge threw the case out saying that 'there is not one scintilla of evidence against this man.' He added: 'His reputation has been dragged through the mud. He leaves the court without a stain on his character.' There was never any stain on my character because I was only guilty of being one of many divorced couples, but for the time being, my 20 year career as a local GP had been ruined and I was poorer by £600,000 — legal costs playing their part here.

Some sort of calm has returned. My other children, themselves devastated by all the upheaval, are on track with their lives. They sturdily resisted pressure from the same professionals to support their sister in untrue allegations although they have all suffered immeasurably under the stress of these events over many years.

After regaining some normality of family life with me, all three are at university and doing very well. I have struggled to rebuild my career against huge adverse odds and am now happily remarried. I spent years in conjunction with ten other locally affected families pursuing the Primary Care Trust and health services to finally get the adolescent unit and its health professionals investigated. Social Services finally did so, apologised and have, belatedly, actually closed the unit down. However Jenny remains estranged from members of her family and emigrated to Australia at the age of 21.

And so, even many years later there remains a void.

26. 'Eileen': arrested, not charged, but condemned to a life sentence (1998 to 2008)

Eileen's account here is based on her presentation at the 2006 AGM of the BFMS. A DVD of the AGM, including Eileen's presentation, can be obtained from the BFMS. Although police and CPS investigations were abandoned in 1998, the quasi-judicial process conducted by the General Medical Council against the psychiatrist was not completed until 2005 when he was found guilty of serious professional misconduct. This part of Eileen's story is related more fully in section 29.3.

I consider myself a normal, law-abiding person living in a civilised country, so therefore nothing could have possibly prepared me for the shock of the police arriving at our doorstep one morning in January 1998, and being arrested on suspicion of sexually abusing my daughter.

I had to go to the toilet, wash and dress in front of the arresting officer. Innocent till proven guilty? Forget it. The treatment I received was degrading and designed to humiliate and intimidate. I was locked up for 13 hours in jail until the police located and questioned our elder son, whom my daughter had also accused. Our house was thoroughly searched. Papers, photos, videos and computer were removed, causing added distress to us and our younger son who was in the middle of 'A' level exams and needed access to the computer for revision. My husband who had been away from home at the time was also arrested and questioned, but two days later.

I didn't enjoy being locked up in jail. How anyone who hasn't committed a crime can cope with being locked up is beyond my comprehension. Fortunately it did not take the police long to realise that our daughter's allegations had no foundation. Indeed, after my interviews one of the officers who had questioned me said, 'I shouldn't say this but ... ' He didn't complete his sentence but I'm sure he was going to say that I had nothing to worry about, that I was not going to be charged.

We did not just sit back and do nothing; we submitted a dossier, in effect our defence, to the police and, after three months of being on bail, learned that we were not going to be charged. In the event, our papers weren't even passed to the Crown Prosecution Service, which is the normal procedure.

Our solicitor said that the police's not sending our papers was the nearest we would get to an apology.

So you may think that's the end of it but my husband and I travel regularly to the USA for his business. Because we've been arrested for a crime of moral turpitude we have to travel on full visas. We're nearly always challenged as to why we travel on full visas and have been told that, if we didn't answer truthfully, telling the immigration officer we have been arrested and accused of sexually abusing our daughter, we would be hauled away for further questioning.

We are always totally truthful about our visas but, even when we do tell the immigration officer what has happened, we are still sometimes subjected to another interview. That is stressful and degrading and something we will have to contend with whenever we travel to the USA.

Our arrests also had another, obvious long-term impact, but on our elder son. He was supposed to be going to the USA for a summer job but could not because of being arrested. Who knows what long-term employment he now might be in if he had been able to go to the USA.

But why did this happen? Why did our daughter make false accusations against us? When she was fifteen our daughter met a faith healer. He made her believe that the reason she was unwell was because of what we, her family, were saying to her and that she would never be well until she had left home and had nothing more to do with us. This caused a great deal of conflict in her mind. She started to see people who were not there. She began to cut herself. She started to be sick. She drank heavily. She smoked and took cannabis. She withdrew from us, her extended family and her friends.

When we finally persuaded her to see a psychiatrist, he, instead of making matters better, made them worse. We believe that at their first meeting, he said to her something along the lines of, 'I know what's wrong with you. You have been sexually abused.' Why do we believe this? She wrote in her diary the day after seeing him for the first time: 'The shrink has got it all wrong. I have not been sexually abused.'

But from that moment, that diagnosis of sexual abuse has impacted very, very strongly on our and our daughter's life. We had no contact with her at all. We did manage to have meetings with her social workers. This caused us further distress.

We had the social workers saying things to us like, 'Even if you've been to court and proved not guilty we would still believe you had sexually abused your daughter.' But, more importantly, it seemed to us that the social workers were doing all they could to reinforce the allegations. What hope was there for our poor daughter?

If she had any doubts as to whether the allegations were true or not, everyone around her was trying to convince her that they were true. Also, the social workers were not prepared to listen to us or accept any information.

They even tampered with her file, shredding pages copied from her diary where she states she has not been abused so that if anybody helping her did have some doubts about the validity of the allegations, important evidence indicating otherwise was missing. This struck us as wrong.

The diagnosis seemed to take on a life of its own. No health care providers could then think of any other reason for our daughter's distress and this means our daughter will never be treated for what is wrong with her because she has been put, wrongly, in this category of an abused victim.

As part of our process of trying to help our daughter we complained. Our complaint to the psychiatrist's NHS Trust was simply brushed aside so we had to complain to the Health Service Ombudsman.

It took nearly three years for their report to come out. Some of the psychiatrist's evidence we could show was not true. We were told that the HSO had to accept what the psychiatrist said. Why? There are factual errors in the report. We pointed this out to the Commissioner and were told that, once the report was written, it could not be rewritten.

The report was shown to the psychiatrist and his NHS Trust before it was finalised so that they could amend it but we were not afforded that privilege. We have received an apology from the psychiatrist's NHS Trust, but the report is inaccurate. The whole system is biased against the innocent.

We also complained to the General Medical Council. That process took seven years. It was very tedious. We had to do a lot of things to make it happen including going to the High Court. Everything was strongly weighted in favour of the psychiatrist. Here is a small example: we were told to limit our evidence to the time in which the psychiatrist treated our daughter. He was allowed to go outside that period.

We were essentially barred from all proceedings at the Hearing, so we could not object to things which we suspected would be inaccurate or misleading. But, despite all of these things, the psychiatrist was actually found guilty of serious professional misconduct, which I suppose is good.

He was not struck off. We were told that amongst the reasons for this was that there are too few psychiatrists in the UK for that to happen.

But what of our daughter? As I say, she has been estranged for 10 years. She was pushed into the arms of the faith healer by the psychiatrist. He is some 40 years her senior and, I believe, totally controlled her. I was in contact with her for a few weeks during the summer of 2006 and then she broke off contact again.

While in contact she told me she had had three miscarriages and she hated the man who had made her pregnant. She is badly bulimic. Her teeth are permanently damaged as a result. She is living in poverty and is not well physically. Her education has been cut short and she is living on benefits.

The good news is that she is now (January 2008) no longer with the healer and we are in touch with her again. She is living with a man 30 years her senior. We don't know if this contact will lead to proper reconciliation but feel the situation is different to 2006. At that time she flatly refused to see her father. She is now very happy to see him.

And she expressed surprise when I said I still loved her, saying, 'Even although I have said dreadful things about you?' So she is fully aware of what she has said. She has said to us that she could quite understand if we no longer loved her. She appears to realise that the healer harmed her. She told us that while with him she was being sick. He said that was because of our influence over her. He was giving her his herbal medicine which he said would stop her being sick but, when she stopped taking it, she stopped being sick.

It's terribly, terribly difficult when something like this happens to you because everything is weighted against you because the authorities simply don't understand. There's this horrible word 'confidentiality.' You are not allowed to impart important information. You can fight the 'system' but you need to fight it for all your worth.

Occasionally you may prevail. Our daughter and we have had a very difficult and distressing decade. Before all this happened we could never have believed such things could happen or that the 'system' could be so against us.

The police did not know how to handle our daughter's allegations. We do not know why they arrested me so aggressively. At my arrest I found out that she had made her allegations some seven months before we were arrested. Why did the police wait so long before doing anything?

They said they were too busy. We were also slightly mystified that they did not want to arrest and question my husband as soon as he became available but think that, after questioning me, the police realised that our daughter's allegations were false. But why did the police simply not just come to us and ask us what had happened instead of coming in so heavy-handed?

They must have known our daughter had been seen by a psychiatrist and had been in a mental hospital and was therefore potentially mentally unstable; so why believe her, particularly as some of her allegations were very extreme? In addition to the ones she made against us she said that her father had drugged her, taken her to the house of one of his friends where he, the friend and several other men, names and numbers unspecified, gang raped her and that the events had been videoed.

It is interesting to note that our daughter became involved with social services three months before we were arrested. Were social workers putting pressure on her? Certainly the social workers we were in touch with seemed to think that if someone says they have been sexually abused, they must have been. Additionally, did her being in a mental hospital contribute to our being arrested? We don't know.

We found it disappointing that the ordinary NHS complaints procedure did not work. It is also a pity that there are failings in both Health Service Commission (later called the Health Service Ombudsman) and GMC procedure.

It is very easy for false memories to be created in vulnerable people and the ensuing results can be absolutely devastating for both the person and their families. Additionally, because of the way the 'system' works, it fails many of the very people it is trying to protect.

All we did over the 10 years was to try and help our daughter. Reconciliation would be a bonus. She now appears to be happy. With our assistance she has started to get better medical help so, hopefully, her health will improve. Only time will tell whether true reconciliation has occurred and we have no idea how to deal with her false allegations. For now they have been consigned to a metaphorical 'box.'

27. The Dawson Family story (late 1990s)

Their daughter's battle to clear her parents' and uncle's names is given in chapter 2 in the form of a legally witnessed statement.

Holly Dawson engaged with the law three times. The first occasion was when she claimed that her father and her uncle had abused her when she was young. The second was when she retracted those accusations.

And the third time was when she went to a solicitor and formally retracted her allegations. When she had first made her allegations she was examined by a doctor at the rape and abuse centre. But her mother knew, for reasons which will be explained later in this article, that she had been a virgin until the age of seventeen.

Despite their eventual total exoneration by Holly, her parents continued to be on the child protection register. Years later, however, her mother, Mrs Gail Dawson, now a widow, insists:

> I just count my blessings. I can't feel sorry for us because we were so lucky that we came out of it. And I'm so proud of Holly that she stood up to those who tried to influence her.

As the saga unfolds one wonders whether the sickness was in the minds of those charged with protecting and treating Holly rather than in her family.

A sequence of events, in which one malign development led to another, began in Holly's GCSE year. She suffered from depression and was referred to a child psychotherapist. While being treated she self-harmed, mainly cutting her arms and legs and the psychotherapist insisted:

> You have been abused and unless you let it out you will never stop self-harming.

Recalling the pressure to remember her childhood, Holly says:

> I was consumed with how I was feeling and couldn't remember anything clearly. To them that was a 'sign' I was repressing abuse.
>
> I started to 'recover' memories of being abused, first by my uncle and later by my mum and dad.

Mrs Dawson comments that she had been increasingly concerned about the effects of her daughter's sessions with the psychotherapist. She told her daughter:

> I can't see how he is helping you because, frequently after you have seen him, you self-harm straight away.

Long before the allegations surfaced, Holly's uncle had died. There was no way her claims could be looked into.

After Holly went to the police the family tragedy switched into higher gear. Holly was taken on three consecutive days to the police rape and abuse suite and questioned. Then, in September 1997, her parents were arrested.

It was a mid morning raid, with two police cars stationed strategically in the area of the family home. One car was spotted by a neighbour as it blocked her drive. The neighbour pointed this out to the driver, who was in plain clothes. He said they would 'not be long'. Mrs Dawson explains:

> They had seen my husband approaching in their mirrors.
>
> The cars pulled out and stopped my husband, who was returning from the shops. There were two policemen in each car. I had been at work nearby and later, as I was leaving to get my car and go to my next job, police were up and down the road knocking on doors. They saw me and asked me to go with them. They said that John was in custody and I would be arrested if I did not accompany them. I objected and asked who would look after our dog.

Mrs Dawson added that they agreed to drive her in the police car to see a neighbour about looking after the dog.

> They also allowed me a quick call to a couple whom I helped with cleaning and shopping. I had to say I wasn't well and couldn't come that morning.

This call was reluctantly permitted and heavily supervised, she said.

Mr Dawson was locked up all day and Mrs Dawson, though not put in a cell, was body-searched. They were questioned separately. 'We left the police station at 6 p.m. on bail and were not allowed to contact Holly in any way.'

This drama had by now developed a momentum of its own. Holly had been persuaded by her child psychotherapist that she had been abused. She had then gone to the police who (as they must) followed up the accusations.

But what was it that made them say, preposterously, to her mother:

> Your daughter's uncle used to pick her up from school and take her home and send her back to you with dirty knickers to wash?

Mrs Dawson says, bluntly:

> Her uncle never picked her up from school. The ideas cannot
> have begun with Holly.

Mrs Dawson believes the ideas were planted in her by her therapists.
'It's not our sort of language,' she says.

Further allegations followed. She said that police said that John would
abuse Holly and that she would stand and watch.

> Your daughter is adamant that he did. And you watched as he
> turned her over and buggered her.

Mrs Dawson comments: 'I didn't truly know what that was.'

At the end of that day of questioning they were released on police bail
on condition that they made no attempt to contact Holly. They were also
banned from seeing her sister's children. 'And it was on learning this,' Mrs
Dawson said, 'that Holly began to realise that what was happening was far
beyond anything she could have thought would happen, as we were a very
close family.'

There was a woman police officer who, Mrs Dawson felt, had viewed the
situation with discreet scepticism from the early days. She rang to say that
Holly had found out from her ex brother-in law about the ban and gone to
the police and said: 'It was not my mum. It was just my dad.' Mrs Dawson
added: 'So, a few days later, I had an official letter saying I was cleared but
not John.'

That was the end of the police ordeal for Mrs Dawson and soon afterwards
the case against John was dropped as well. It was three months before they
had any contact with Holly. But she and her mother are glad that this was
in time for her to be reconciled with her parents before John died, in 2000,
Mrs Dawson says:

> I just count my blessings. I can't feel sorry for us because we
> were so, so lucky that we came out of it.

She continued:

> Holly was sent to Devon where she was taken into care by a retired
> vicar and his wife on 30th November 1997. On 17th December
> this vicar rang us to ask whether he could possibly bring Holly
> to visit, as he felt there was such a lot that didn't make sense or
> add up. Of course we said 'yes.'

Holly recalls:

> My dad held out his arms and said 'Can I have a hug?' I fell
> sobbing into them. How could I have thought he had hurt me?

Her mother adds:

> That was the start of building bridges. We just thank God that
> she went to stay with the vicar and his wife, as they really helped
> Holly on the way back.

In the family reunions which followed Holly's return she heard for the first
time of the condition called False Memory. To her it made sense of what had
happened. 'I'd gone to therapy with depression and come out convinced my
dad had raped me. I'd never been abused. All those "flashbacks" weren't
real,' she said

The vicar contacted a solicitor on Holly's behalf to whom Holly gave a
witnessed statement of exoneration of her parents and her aunt and late
uncle. Copies of this were sent to social services, police, doctors, Holly's
psychotherapist and Holly's aunt. A copy was also sent, via the solicitor, to
the ex husband of Holly's sister.

Mrs Dawson said:

> Through our solicitor we sent, along with Holly's exoneration,
> an accompanying letter to the psychotherapist, saying we hoped
> lessons had been learned and other parents would not have to go
> through what we had been through.

The psychotherapist replied (in part):

> I truly hope that what Holly says in her statement is self-motivated.
> I fear that someone has put pressure on her to change her mind,
> and that she is in the process of shutting off lots of her experience
> and memory in order to comply.

Mrs Dawson comments:

> He was concerned as to 'who had changed her mind.'

We wanted to write back to him but our solicitor advised against it. She
continued:

> We also had a very nice letter from the police, in which the po-
> licewoman added a comment at the bottom saying how pleased
> she was for us. And there was a lovely letter from the surgery
> where John and I received counselling to help us through the very
> bad days.

Mrs Dawson said that their ex son-in-law (Holly's ex brother in law) had
once, in earlier years, been a great help with Holly.

But unfortunately, later on he believed we had abused her and it was because of him we couldn't see the grandchildren, as he and our daughter by now were divorced. He also told social services that I had a niece with four children who visited us.

Social services told them (this was while we were on bail) that they had to have no contact with us.

My niece said 'I trust my aunt and uncle 100% and will still visit.' But they were told that if they did the children might be taken away from them.

Mrs Dawson said she and her husband had received a reply from their ex son-in-law to the solicitor's letter which had accompanied their copy of Holly's exoneration. They had felt it to be hostile and unsympathetic. It said (in part):

In thinking about your letter and what I did I have reached the conclusion, which I do not expect either of you to share, that I am not the cause of your distress and that whilst I understand why you are hurt and angry I am not willing to be a scapegoat for it.

Mrs Dawson said that at one stage during Holly's teenage years and while she was still self-harming she had been so worried about her that, against her own conscience, she had read Holly's diary.

I told the policeman and policewoman that Holly was a virgin until about the age of 17 as I had read her diary (it wrote of a relationship with a male friend at that time). The policewoman asked where the diaries were and I said Holly had them.

Mrs Dawson added:

I've recently discovered from Holly that the police did take her diaries away and now I'm wondering if what was said there led to John's case being dropped.

About two years ago I rang my ex son-in-law to ask if I could see him as I needed to talk to him. He came and I asked him if he really knew the pain and heartache we had gone through.

We talked about various things, some he couldn't remember. When he left I said to him: 'Do you honestly believe that we abused Holly?' His reply was, 'Well, something must have happened.' I felt as if I had been stabbed.

John didn't want him at his funeral but, through his ex-wife he said that if his boys needed him — they were nine and ten years old — he would come. His parents assured me they would watch him and leave the church right after the service. Thank God he never came. He is a counsellor himself now.

Speaking of her husband's death three years later Mrs Dawson said:

If she hadn't come back to us I don't know how we would have coped.

Holly said:

My mum and I are fine now. In a lot of ways our relationship has changed for the better. The memories felt real and I had no reason to doubt them at the time but I now know they were false. I had problems and this was a solution.

Mrs Dawson said:

This Easter Holly and I went to Spring Harvest (a Christian festival). One session was on self-harm. Holly spoke so well. The people in our groups came and gave her a hug and thanked her for sharing this. They also thanked me for sharing what I went through as a parent.

I am so lucky. It is something you can never forget. I have some health problems now and Holly is always sending cards and offering to help and saying how sorry she is. But it was never her fault. We are so very, very lucky.

Part V.

Disciplinary hearings

28. Cases heard by counselling and therapy representative bodies

Although the Health Professions Council (HPC) has put forward proposals for the regulation of Counselling and Psychotherapy these are unlikely to receive government approval before 2011 and, most probably, much later (see summary of the HPC's proposals in chapter 8). At the time of publication it was not, therefore, possible to obtain reports of disciplinary hearings published by a single, unified, enforceable and public disciplinary process similar to that of the GMC and HPC.

This absence in this book of published accounts of disciplinary actions by therapy bodies following complaints against their members does not, therefore, indicate a high level of satisfaction among clients who have sought the services of a therapist or counsellor. Rather it is testimony to the failure of the organisations to which they belong to place the interests of the clients above those of their members, and the continued resistance by many to the introduction of a meaningful regulatory system — a view supported by the words of HPC Chief Executive, Marc Seale,

> Statutory regulation would seek to enhance public protection by protecting commonly recognised professional titles and providing a fair and appropriate complaints system. It would also seek to protect the professionals by removing incompetent and unethical practitioners from practising and potentially harming the public, and thus reducing damage to the industry's reputation [Health Professions Council, 2009b].

29. Cases heard by the General Medical Council's Fitness to Practise Panel

*In view of the length of the transcript of the hearing against Dr Eastgate —
over 70 pages — the report has been limited to the statements of charges on
day 1 and the Committee's Determination on the final day. A full transcript
of Dr Eastgate's hearing, excluding sessions held* in camera, *can be read on
the BFMS website. The hearing against Dr Spender took place* in camera
and the report, below, is of the Determination only.

*For legal reasons, the book's editors have been advised against expressing
views on the conduct and outcome of the hearings. However, the parents who
brought the case against Dr Eastgate agreed that their article [A, 2004] could
be reproduced as section 29.2.*

29.1. Dr John Eastgate (2003 to 2006)

The Charges

THE COMMITTEE SECRETARY: The Committee will inquire into the following
charge against John William Eastgate: That, being registered under the
Medical Act,

1. At all material times you were a consultant in adolescent psychiatry at
   the Princess Margaret Hospital, Swindon (the Hospital);

2.

   a. On 13 June 1996 Miss A (date of birth . . .) was admitted to the
      Hospital and on 27 June to the adolescent unit,

   b. At all material times you were the consultant in charge of Miss
      A's care;

3.

   a. On 9 July 1996 you held an individual session with Miss A in
      which you,

145

          i. assisted Miss A to identify the person who "had let her down",

          ii. asked whether "it happened once or a number of occasions",

          iii. asked Miss A "when she first felt uncomfortable",

    b. Your questions and comments relating to the above were,

          i. inappropriate,

          ii. unprofessional;

4.

    a. In the afternoon of 9 July 1996 you held a further individual session with Miss A in which you,

          i. told Miss A that what Professor X had done sounded wrong,

          ii. told Miss A that you were "worried that he may have done it to other children as well",

    b. Your comments relating to the above were,

          i. inappropriate,

          ii. unprofessional;

5. You failed to keep a verbatim account of your interviews with Miss A on

    a. 9 July 1996 (afternoon session),

    b. 10 July 1996 (11.15am),

    c. 10 July 1996 (5pm),

    d. 11 July 1996 (9.30am),

    e. 15 July 1996,

    f. 16 July 1996,

    g. on or about 19 July 1996;

6.

    a. You reported the allegations made by Miss A in relation to Professor X to the Child Protection Team,

          i. without first having taken reasonable steps to verify their truth or otherwise,

          ii. without first sharing your concerns with the parents of Miss A,

    b. Your conduct in this regard was,

    i. inappropriate,

    ii. unprofessional;

And in relation to the facts alleged you have been guilty of serious professional misconduct.

The Determination

THE CHAIRMAN: Dr Eastgate: This case goes to the heart of a doctor's dilemma in circumstances when, whatever he or she does, criticism and controversy is likely to follow; situations in which there may be no absolute truth, no perfect answers; moments which may come out of the blue, imposing huge new urgent demands on an already full clinical week. Conflicting interests and responsibilities must be balanced; decisions must be taken in the best interests of patients, balancing all the circumstances and conflicting interests at the time. The doctor has to have the courage of his or her own convictions.

The Committee have heard that in such circumstances neither the GMC nor the courts would blame a doctor for acting in good faith and in the best interests of a patient, provided his or her decision was based upon sound clinical evaluation and judgment.

On the other hand, any doctor may be required to justify his or her professional decision. Such justification has been your task at this hearing.

In assessing all the written and oral evidence, the Committee have had the benefit of expert evidence from three eminent child and adolescent psychiatrists. In essence, the two experts called by your counsel took the view that you had acted appropriately; the expert called by the counsel for the complainants took a different view. The two experts, who agreed in general, did not, however, agree in every particular. One expert, Dr Alyson Hall, commented that in this controversial field of possible sexual abuse of a child, that the Committee might receive as many different opinions as there were experts, saying:

> ... you could get 10 experts in this room and you would find us all having different views about this case and how it should be handled. My view is, for what it is worth and I do not want to be dogmatic, to say that there is no right way, that there are just better ways and worse ways and that we have to try and do our best in these very difficult cases.

The Committee have, therefore, listened carefully to all three experts and used their own, partly clinical, common sense to decide which opinion to prefer in respect to each detail of the charge. The Committee have been assisted in their findings of fact by all the experts.

The Committee have given detailed consideration to all the evidence adduced in this case, and have taken account of the submissions made by counsel and the advice given by the Legal Assessor. They have borne in mind that the burden of proof rests on the Complainant and that the standard of proof required is that they should be sure.

They have considered each head and sub-head of charge separately. Certain facts have been proved against you. However, the Committee have found that they would be insufficient to support a finding of serious professional misconduct.

These are the findings on the facts in relation to Heads of Charge 1–5:

> 1 and 2 were admitted and found proved.
>
> 3. a. On 9 July 1996 you held an individual session with Miss A in which you,
>
> > i. assisted Miss A to identify the person who "had let her down", was found proved.
> >
> > ii. asked whether "it happened once or a number of occasions", was found proved.
> >
> > iii. asked Miss A "when she first felt uncomfortable", was found proved.
>
> b. Your questions and comments relating to the above were,
>
> > i. inappropriate, not found proved
> >
> > ii. unprofessional; not found proved.
>
> 4. a. In the afternoon of 9 July 1996 you held a further individual session with Miss A in which you,
>
> > i. told Miss A that what Professor X had done sounded wrong, Found proved.
> >
> > ii. told Miss A that you were "worried that he may have done it to other children as well", Found proved.
>
> b. Your comments relating to the above were,
>
> > i. inappropriate, Not found proved in relation to 4a.i., but found proved in relation to 4a.ii.
> >
> > ii. unprofessional; Not found proved in relation to 4a.i., but found proved in relation to 4a.ii.

The Committee were not satisfied that your conduct in your interview with Miss A on the morning of July 9 was either inappropriate or unprofessional;

they were very aware of the danger of misinterpretation by hindsight of the significance of the use of particular words or phrases. On the other hand, they found your conduct in the interview with Miss A on the afternoon of July 9 was inappropriate and unprofessional because it was likely immediately to strengthen her impression that she might have been improperly touched at medical examination. They had regard to your note that Miss A was "surprised when I suggested that not only did it sound wrong to me but I was worried that he may have done it to other children". They heard your explanation but considered that, in the light of all the evidence, your comments on that occasion were inappropriate and unprofessional.

These are the findings in relation to head of charge 5:

> You failed to keep an account of your interviews with Miss A which was as nearly verbatim as possible on — and you will see that the head of charge has been amended by the Committee. There are a number of dates here:

> a. Found proved;
> b. Found proved;
> c. Found proved;
> d. Found proved;
> e. Found proved;
> f. Found proved;
> g. Found proved.

Two of the medical experts considered, and indeed you yourself admitted in evidence before the Committee, that the quality of your notes at the crucial period of the afternoon of July 9 to on or about July 19 was unsatisfactory. The Committee found your notes were inadequate, either as a record of events assisting understanding of the revelation of her concern regarding possible inappropriate touching or for assisting clinical care when another consultant took over in your absence on holiday. The Committee were persuaded by the evidence of Professor Zeitlin, Dr Eyre and indeed your own admission. They noted that you were aware of the importance of good notes, having written on July 16, that "It is important that all discussions, whether with nursing staff or other clinical staff, are written down as near verbatim as possible". You failed to follow your own good advice. The Committee accepted the argument that nobody could ever produce a literally verbatim account without mechanical recording. Therefore, they found the facts in Head 5 proved to the lesser extent defined by the words of your own note of July 16.

These are the findings in relation to head of charge 6:

6. a. You caused to be reported the allegations made by Miss A in relation to Professor X to the Child Protection Team, was admitted and found proved as amended above.

   i. without first having taken reasonable steps to verify their truth or otherwise; not found proved.

   ii. without first sharing your concerns with the parents of Miss A, had already been admitted and found proved.

   b. Your conduct in this regard was,

   i. inappropriate, not found proved.

   ii. unprofessional, not found proved.

As a doctor very experienced in matters of sexual abuse of children, you concluded on the clinical evidence at the time that you had an overriding professional duty to share your concerns with the senior social worker on the Child Protection Team, without having first consulted Miss A's parents. You were concerned with the possibility of other children being at risk, and were fully aware of the possible harm to Miss A, her family and Professor X.

You knew that it is good practice to keep the parents closely involved and indeed it appears from an entry in your diary on July 9 that you had planned to telephone Mrs A in London. The senior social worker, Mr Evans, with whom you conferred on July 12, was strongly of the opinion that the parents should not be involved until after a strategy meeting had been held. He also made it clear in evidence to the Committee that he would have taken matters into his own hands as a result of his assessment of your information, even if you had not agreed together that a strategy meeting was necessary. Contrary to his advice, you used your own clinical judgment and spoke with Mrs A that same evening.

The medical experts were sharply divided in their opinion as to whether you should have shared your concerns with Miss A's parents before consulting with Mr Evans. The Committee in all the circumstances did not find your conduct in this regard to be either inappropriate or unprofessional. They accepted that in the end you had to use your own clinical judgment.

Having regard to the facts admitted and found proved against you, the Committee consider that taking all the facts and circumstances into account, your conduct at the interview on the afternoon of July 9 and your note-taking then and on the subsequent days fell short of the principles of good practice in this sensitive and difficult situation. However, they consider that these limited failings seen in the light of your previously unblemished record, could not amount to the grave finding of serious professional misconduct.

That concludes the case.

29.2. One family's experience of complaining to the GMC (1998 to 2005)

The following article by Mr and Mrs A, the parents involved in bringing the above case before the GMC's Professional Conduct Committee was published in the June 2004 BFMS Newsletter.

The transcript of the General Medical Council's (GMC) Professional Conduct Committee hearing of the complaint by Mr & Mrs A against Dr John W. Eastgate, MRCPsych, DCH in September 2003 may be found on the BFMS web-site. Anyone considering making a complaint against a Child & Adolescent Psychiatrist would be well advised to study it. This note is intended merely to explain some of the procedures involved.

The legal processes in the family courts, the NHS Trusts' complaints procedure and the GMC vary widely and must be understood together with the motivation of those involved.

In the family courts the protection of the child overrides all other considerations. The rules of evidence are lax — hearsay evidence is admitted for instance — and the test applied is the 'balance of probabilities.' In practice the desire of officials to avoid blame in the event of a mistake means the process is heavily loaded against the parents, with prosecution medical expert evidence too readily accepted at face value. The difficulties of engaging one's own expert have been well highlighted in Parliament by Vera Baird QC MP (Hansard, February 24th 2004, essential reading). This should only be approached with extreme care — but without a conflicting opinion the judge is left without much option but to go along with the prosecution's expert.

It is as the employer of the doctor that the NHS Trust processes a complaint. There is a conflict of interest between its duty as a trustee of public funds and its responsibility to supervise safe and effective practice by its employees. Given the consequent financial liability there is an extreme reluctance to admit fault. While the rapid timetable laid down appears to be adhered to, too often it merely leads to a rapid comprehensive whitewash. To all intents and purposes the NHS complaints system is totally ineffective in the resolution of complex complaints.

The GMC is the (self) regulatory body with which doctors must be registered in order to practise medicine and a complaint may lead to the doctor being struck off the register if found guilty of serious professional misconduct, or to a lesser sanction being applied such as compulsory re-training. The legal hurdles in the process are very high indeed. The hearing is conducted to criminal trial rules, hearsay evidence is not admissible and the test employed is 'beyond reasonable doubt' — the panel must be 'sure.' Following the determination of a hearing the doctor has 28 days to appeal and as of early 2004 a new body, the Council for Healthcare Regulatory Excellence , has 28 days to appeal against excessive leniency with the power to reverse this. But in practice many of those doctors who are struck off with attendant publicity are quietly re-admitted within a few months.

The GMC's filtering process is well explained on their web-site. A medically qualified screener presides over the progress of the complaint with assistance from a screener who is a lay member, while the leg work and all communication with the complainants is done by the administration staff. Establishing a good relationship with them is vital, and they should be treated with the utmost courtesy. Frustrations are best taken out on your legal advisors.

Nearly four years elapsed while the GMC considered whether to refer the case against Dr Eastgate to a public hearing by the Professional Conduct Committee. The Preliminary Proceedings Committee, sitting behind closed doors, tried to reject it. However a factual error by this committee meant that it was possible to contest this decision through an application for judicial review, which caused the GMC to change it's mind — at huge financial cost to all.

Having decided to refer the case on, we were offered the choice of using the GMC's own legal advisors and leaving the case entirely in their hands, or using our own team largely at the GMC's expense. After our experiences so far we had no hesitation in choosing to manage the case ourselves. This involved the selection of Leading Counsel experienced in GMC work and an expert witness (see above). The opinion of any expert(s) appointed would be disclosed to the defence irrespective of our views on it, so it was important to make the right choice. The medical notes were now made available to us for the first time and were examined by the chosen expert, Professor Harry Zeitlin. His views played the dominant role in formulating the charges against Dr Eastgate.

There were three broad themes to the charges laid against Dr Eastgate. These involved the manner in which he had questioned Miss A about her medical examinations by a consultant paediatrician, whether he had taken adequate notes of these sessions, and whether he should have consulted Mr & Mrs A about the circumstances of the medical examinations before reporting allegations about the paediatrician to the Child Protection Team. These were all matters entirely confined to the medical profession and it is significant that Professor X, the consultant paediatrician involved, agreed to give evidence for the prosecution. *These events occurred in the very early stages of the treatment of Miss A by Dr Eastgate and while it may be probable that they led directly to more serious matters which occurred later, proof to the required standard did not exist in the medical notes to prove causation.*

In September 2003, over six years after the lodging of the original complaint, the hearing commenced in the imposing surroundings of the GMC's

Council chamber. There was intense press interest. The case itself turned on the expert evidence. Professor Zeitlin argued tenaciously for the prosecution, Dr Alyson Hall and Dr Arnon Bentovim would not agree to any criticism of Dr Eastgate. Both the latter were accused of bias by the prosecution counsel. And that was that. In their determination the panel found that:

- While certain facts had been proved, 'they would be insufficient to amount to a finding of serious professional misconduct.'

- Certain comments in Dr Eastgate's interviewing of Miss A were found to have been 'unprofessional and inappropriate.'

- And most importantly, they found that Dr Eastgate's conduct in an interview with Miss A 'was inappropriate and unprofessional because it was likely immediately to strengthen her impression that she might have been improperly touched at medical examination.'

- Further comments in the same interview were found to have been 'inappropriate and unprofessional.'

- Dr Eastgate's notes of seven separate interviews with Miss A were found to have been 'inadequate.'

- Dr Eastgate's failure to have shared his concerns with Miss A's parents before consulting the child protection team, although admitted, was not found to have been inappropriate or unprofessional. This was disappointing but not altogether unexpected.

Dr Eastgate was brought to account for himself in the Council chamber of the GMC only by the courage, tenacity and financial resources of Mr and Mrs A. This was a case that the GMC would rather have avoided. Indeed it was based on a paradox — the only evidence was contained in medical notes that were found to be 'inadequate' on seven different occasions. It is to be hoped that it will have helped to persuade child and adolescent psychiatrists that they cannot behave as Dr Eastgate did with impunity, and that they too will be named and shamed if they were to do so.

29.3. Dr Quentin Wynn Spender (2005)

Fitness to Practise Panel Hearing
New case of conduct heard under the Preliminary Proceedings Committee
and Professional Conduct Committee (Procedure) Rules 1988
Session beginning on 16 May 2005
London

The Determination

Dr Spender

At all material times you were a senior lecturer and Consultant in Child and Adolescent Psychiatry in an NHS Trust in Sussex, practising from The Child and Family Service for Mental Health, John Grenville House, Chichester and also at Orchard House, Chichester.

In July 1996 you saw a Miss A in your capacity as Consultant Psychiatrist. Thereafter between July 1996 and August 1997 Miss A was under your care as regards her mental health. You have admitted that by 14 April 1997 you had formed the view that Miss A had been subjected to sexual abuse by some or all of the members of her family. The Panel found that you had insufficient information on which to draw that conclusion. In reaching that decision, the Panel noted that there was some evidence implicating members of Miss A's family but it was satisfied that you had insufficient evidence to draw the conclusion that Miss A had been sexually abused by some or all members of her family.

The Panel also found that you failed to have any or any sufficient regard to other sources of information apart from the evidence emanating directly or indirectly from Miss A and failed to make the necessary enquiries to put yourself in a position from which you could safely draw such a conclusion. In reaching those findings, the Panel was satisfied that you should have kept an open mind about the possible causes of Miss A's difficulties and that you should have had greater regard for other sources of information. The Panel noted the evidence of Dr McArdle, the GMC's expert witness, who stated that a strong statement requires strong evidence. The Panel was satisfied that you did not adequately explore other sources of information or make appropriate enquiries before drawing the conclusion that you did and making what the Panel found to be a strong statement. The Panel was not assisted by the evidence of your own expert, Dr Bentovim on this point.

You admitted that on 14 April 1997 you had a meeting with Dr and Mrs B at which you stated that you believed that Miss A had been sexually abused by some or all members of her family. In a letter dated 1 May 1997 written to Dr G, Miss A's general practitioner, and copied to Ms LA, a senior social worker, Dr and Mrs B and Miss A, you wrote:

> Miss A's parents and I had a major disagreement about the development of A's current problems. I believe that this (is) at least in part due to sexual abuse by some or all family members.

The Panel found that your conduct in making the assertions that you did orally on 14 April 1997 and in writing by letter dated 1 May 1997 was inappropriate, irresponsible and unprofessional. In reaching these findings, the Panel was satisfied you should have foreseen the possible adverse consequences of the inappropriate wording you used in your letter dated 1 May 1997. The Panel considered that a responsible Consultant Child and Adolescent Psychiatrist would have been more circumspect in expressing the conclusions you had reached.

In about late 1998 and/or early 1999 there was an episode of bullying at a school in West Sussex ('The School') in which a group of three boys bullied another boy, Master X. Among the group of bullies was Master Y (the aged 13).

In March 1999 Boy X made an allegation that Boy Y had sexually assaulted him in the toilets at the school. On 10 March 1999 the Head Teacher, Mr W, excluded Boy Y from the school for 13 days and that period was subsequently extended.

Mr W called a meeting for professionals on 10 May 1999 to review the decision to exclude Boy Y and to consider future arrangements for both Boys X and Y.

You attended the meeting of 10 May 1999. At that meeting you expressed *inter alia* broadly your opinion that Boy X was not only physically abused, but also sexually abused; that you assumed that the perpetrator of the sexually abuse as well as the physical bullying was Boy Y; that the probability was that Boy Y had himself been sexually abused and that the probability was high that without professional help Boy Y would abuse another victim.

On 11 May 1999 Mr W decided to exclude Boy Y permanently from the school, because he believed, on the balance of probabilities, having listened to the various professional agencies, including yourself, that Boy X had been sexually abused by Boy Y.

In a letter dated 21 May 1999 to Mr W you set out your opinion that Boy X was not only physically abused, but also sexually abused; that you assumed that the perpetrator of the sexual abuse as well as the physical bullying was Boy Y; that the probability that Boy Y had himself been sexually abused was 75%; that the probability that he was the perpetrator of the abuse on Boy X was at least 95%; that the probability of Boy Y having been abused in some way was at least 90%; that the probability was very high indeed that without professional help Boy Y would abuse another victim.

The Panel found that in forming and expressing a view as to the likelihood that Boy Y had sexually abused Boy X, you had insufficient information before drawing that conclusion. In reaching this finding the Panel was satisfied that you had insufficient evidence upon which to express the likelihood that Boy Y had abused Boy X in terms of a specific percentage probability.

The Panel also found that you made assertions of fact which were based upon uncorroborated allegations. In considering this allegation, the Panel took the view that it dealt with a purely factual matter. While the allegations made by Boy X in relation to Boy Y were strong, they were nevertheless uncorroborated. This finding implied no criticism of you.

In forming and expressing a view as to the likelihood that Boy Y had himself been abused and/or sexually abused you had insufficient information to make those assertions. In reaching this finding, the Panel was satisfied that the research on which you relied could not substantiate the specific probability of 90% that you asserted.

The Panel found that your conduct in making the assertions that you did at a meeting on 10 May 1999 and in a letter dated 21 May 1999 was inappropriate, irresponsible and unprofessional. In reaching these findings the Panel took account of the admissions that you made in respect of what you said at the meetings on 10 May 1999 and the content on your letter dated 21 May 1999 and its own determination that you had insufficient information in drawing your conclusion about the likelihood that Boy Y had sexually abused Boy X. It also took account of its findings that you had insufficient evidence on which to make those assertions. Further, the Panel is satisfied that you were irresponsible in not considering the potential repercussions of your actions when you went beyond the terms of reference of the request for a report from the Headmaster of the school in framing the letter of 21 May 1999. The Panel considered that there were more appropriate and professional methods of bringing your concern for Boy Y to the attention of the appropriate authorities. In reaching its decision the Panel also noted that Boy Y was not your patient and that you had not seen him.

The Panel has considered all the evidence, including the expert and character evidence provided by eminent professionals working in the field of Paediatrics and Child and Adolescent Psychiatry. It acknowledges that this area of medicine in which you practise is complex and has noted the evidence in your support that the nature of your work brings with it a high risk of complaint by some parties. Nevertheless the Panel is concerned that in forming your opinion on these cases, in the case of Miss A you failed to explore other avenues of inquiry and in both cases you had insufficient information before drawing your conclusions. The Panel is also concerned that, in expressing your views as you did both orally and in writing in both cases, you did not take account of the possible effect of your assertions on the recipients and the families of Miss A and Boy Y.

A doctor has a position of trust in society and the Panel considers that it is essential that any letters or reports prepared by a medical practitioner, especially by a consultant should be constructed carefully and with proper consideration for the subject matter and its possible effects on the reader. As regards your letter dated 21 May 1999 in relation to Boy Y, you should have realised that because your opinion could influence the decision taken by the group of professionals receiving your report, you had a duty to be precise in expressing your concern and any views about Boy Y. The Panel has noted that paragraph 41 of the October 1995 edition of 'Good Medical Practice' and paragraph 55 of the July 1998 edition, which were in effect at the respective times of the two incidents, both state that registered medical practitioners must take reasonable steps to verify any statement before signing a document. The Panel considers that on the basis of the way in which you arrived at and expressed your assertions about Miss A and Boy Y, both orally and in your two letters, your conduct fell seriously short of this standard. Further, at no time in these proceedings have you acknowledged that there may have been failings in your conduct.

Taking all of the above matters into account and noting that there have been two separate incidents, the Panel is satisfied that your conduct amounts to a serious departure from the standards expected of a registered medical practitioner and finds you guilty of serious professional misconduct.

In considering whether to take action in relation to your registration, the Panel has considered the issue of proportionality and has balanced the interests of the public against your own. The Panel has given careful consideration to the submissions made on your behalf by Mr Finucane, those made on behalf of the GMC by Mr Kark and the advice given by the Legal Assessor. It has also considered carefully the GMC's Indicative Sanctions Guidance, dated May 2004.

The Panel has read the large number of testimonials and character references from your professional colleagues as well as those from patients and their parents, and there is no doubt that you are regarded as a committed, caring and very hardworking doctor and that the eminent professional colleagues who have provided testimonials hold you in high esteem.

In determining the appropriate sanction in your case, the Panel first considered whether it would be sufficient to conclude your case with a reprimand. The Panel is conscious of its duty to protect the interests of patients and the public interest. Based upon all the material it has considered during this hearing, the Panel is satisfied that there is no risk to patient safety. Accordingly, the Panel is satisfied that it would be both appropriate and proportionate to conclude this case with a reprimand.

The Panel might have gone on to consider a more serious sanction but in reaching its decision paid particular regard to the length of the delay in bringing this case to a hearing which has taken place eight and a half and six and a half years after the events. The Panel has taken into account the fact that you have continued in the same area of clinical practice and that there has been no evidence of any repetition of the conduct that has brought you before it. Nevertheless, in these two cases you demonstrated a high-handed and blinkered approach to your work. In the case of Miss A you gave your conclusion in unnecessarily blunt terms to Miss A's parents. In the case of Boy Y you showed a lack of professional judgment in not simply providing Mr W with the information he required to support the decision that he proposed to take, and separately in bringing your concerns with regard to Boy Y to the appropriate authorities in measured terms. The Panel considered that you failed to have due consideration for the families concerned or the likely impact upon them of the information that you were imparting.

The case is now concluded.

30. Case heard by the British Psychological Society's Conduct Committee: Mrs Janet Sinclair (2007)

The following report was first published in the March 2008 edition of the BFMS Newsletter. It predates the transfer of regulatory responsibility for practising psychologists to the Health Professions Council (HPC).

The British Psychological Society's (BPS) disciplinary notice in the December 2007 edition of their journal, *The Psychologist* [British Psychological Society, 2007], raised our interest and approval.

After many unsuccessful attempts over the years by accused parents to gain recognition from the BPS of their complaints about the unsafe practice of a few psychologists, finally, in October 2007, one of the BPS's Graduate members was disciplined for breaching the Society's Code of Conduct regarding the use of hypnosis. For failing to inform her client of the advantages and disadvantages of hypnosis, recommend alternative methods of therapy and advise her client that no technique can reliably recover memories, Mrs Janet Sinclair was found in breach of Clauses 1 and 5.1 of the Code of Conduct. In addition, she was in breach of Sections 9 and 14 of the *Guidelines for Psychologists Working with Clients in Contexts in Which Issues Related to Recovered Memories May Arise* [British Psychological Society, 2000] for failing to avoid being drawn into searching for memories of abuse and failing to avoid engaging in activities and techniques that are intended to reveal indications of past sexual abuse of which the client had no memory.

Mrs Sinclair was severely reprimanded with a condition on her membership that in any future consultations involving hypnosis with a client she must take full notes and present them to her supervisor whilst also presenting her signed supervision notes to the Society on a quarterly basis.

Part VI.

Justice for the falsely accused third party

Introduction to Part VI

In a small number of cases known to the BFMS, retractors have success-fully obtained compensation from practitioners of regression therapies. The case of Jim Fairlie and his daughter Katrina, reported below, highlights the problems faced by falsely accused third parties in obtaining redress. In this article, the position under Scottish Law is clearly stated in the ruling by Judge Lord Kingarth.

31. Civil Court hearing in Britain: the Fairlie Case (1994 to 2007)

What happened to the Fairlie family could happen to any family

Background

In 2004 Jim Fairlie, a former Scottish National Party Deputy Leader, failed on legal technicalities, in his long and financially crippling actions for third party damages against Perth and Kinross Healthcare NHS Trust and the Social Work Department — actions that followed his daughter Katrina's admission to hospital in 1994 for treatment for stomach pains when, after being seen by a consultant psychiatrist, she allegedly 'recovered' memories of having been sexually abused by her father and 17 other men, including two MPs, and beating to death a six year old girl — allegations she later recognised as false.

The story of Katrina's referral to hospital in 1994 for stomach pains, the misdiagnosis of her illness and her subsequent psychiatric treatment, how she came to report her 'recovered' memories to the police and social services, the disastrous effect on the family and her father's career, his long and frustrating fight to obtain answers and redress, and Katrina's very limited success in her legal action, ended in 2007 and cost Jim Fairlie nearly £200,000.

> After I was informed of the allegations, it took three months of daily calls to the Social Work Department (SWD), sometimes twice per day, before the person in charge of the enquiry agreed to meet me in December 1995,

said Fairlie.

> Every word of the conversation was noted by a scribe but every question I asked received the same answer, 'no comment'. When the notes were produced by the SWD, all that was recorded was, 'Mr Fairlie was given general information.'

The original notes had been lost.

Further meetings followed. The Press and family were informed. He complained to the Director of Law and Administration about the conduct of the SWD. He agreed to hold an internal enquiry. There were further delays with no explanation given to Fairlie for the delay. After several weeks in the dark he telephoned the lawyer in charge of the enquiry and was advised that he had submitted his report to the SWD. They refused to give Fairlie a copy and said that 'all social work personnel had acted appropriately.'

As the matter was now public, Fairlie made his views on the SWD's handling of the case clear in letters to the press, inviting them to take legal action for libel but none resulted.

By then the police had decided not to pursue the case but the damage had already been done. He was confronted by the family and Fairlie and his wife spent their first Christmas after the allegations were made on their own, separated from their children. The suggestion was made at the time of wider family abuse; the sons were not informed of the police and SWD enquiry because, 'as they had been brought up in a culture of abuse, they could also be abusers,' while the eldest daughter was contacted as she might have been a victim.

Katrina's story of her misdiagnosis — and the consequences

Jim Fairlie writes:

> The medical team misdiagnosed Katrina's stomach pains from day one. They removed her appendix and found there was nothing wrong with it. The pains continued and three weeks later they removed her gall bladder, and the information given to us the day after, and the information contained in her medical and psychiatric notes from then on, was that there was nothing wrong with the gall bladder either — no pathology found. It was only when we managed to get the medical notes two and a half years later as evidence in our action for damages that we discovered the Lab Report, showing that Katrina had had severe cholecystitis. The relevance of that report appears to have been overlooked in informing Katrina's treatment.

> Katrina was released from Perth Royal Infirmary (PRI) with a wound so severely infected that a nurse was required to make daily visits for the first two weeks after her release. She was prescribed Pethidine for the pain, which continued unabated, for the next six months, by which time she had become addicted

166

to the drug. Professor Sydney Brandon who agreed to be the 'expert witness' at the legal actions that followed pointed out in his report to the court that Pethidine was an inappropriate drug to use with someone who has had gall bladder problems. This was later confirmed by Dr Janet Boakes who took the place of Professor Brandon after his death.

Our own GP was so concerned that he insisted Katrina be re-admitted to PRI for further tests and for addiction to the drug. Remember at this time the medical team were still insisting that there had been nothing wrong with Katrina's gall bladder and further examination concentrated on a physical cause of her pain. When this was not found, it was assumed that her condition was psychosomatic, hence her admission to Murray Royal Hospital (MRH), which is a psychiatric hospital, where she was subjected to therapy that caused the damage.

Katrina spent 15 months at MRH being treated by a psychiatrist, two psychologists and a nurse, using a form of therapy involving mind-altering drugs and prolonged interviews. Her mental health deteriorated rapidly and her weight dropped to six and a half stone. She attempted suicide. Her nightmares turned into hallucinations and she began to recall allegedly 'forgotten' experiences of her father raping her at the age of two, running a paedophile ring with seventeen other men, including two MPs and beating to death a six year old girl — all allegations she later recognised as false.

When Katrina discharged herself from Murray Royal Hospital after 15 months she was still in need of psychiatric care, given the treatment to which she had been subjected and the turmoil it had created. Our own GP, after consultation with colleagues, suggested the Cullen Centre, an annexe of Edinburgh Royal Infirmary (ERI). The discharge letter from Murray Royal Hospital said that Katrina suffered from anorexia, among other things, and the unit dealt with eating disorders. Over a ten month period, Katrina was treated an as outpatient of ERI, after which she was admitted to the Priory in Roehampton where she spent the next year. It was only during that stay that we discovered Katrina was being subjected to similar therapy techniques and had begun making the same accusations in her journals. When she finally discharged herself, again against medical advice, she moved into her own flat in Perth and has been on her own and looking after herself ever since. It was only after she had cut herself off from the therapists, something Dr Boakes had suggested she should do some months earlier, that Katrina began the road to recovery.

The Fairlie family's fight for justice

The story of the quest for justice by Jim and Katrina Fairlie falls into three parts:

   i. Jim Fairlie's action against the Social Work Department

  ii. Jim Fairlie's action against Perth and Kinross Healthcare NHS Trust

 iii. daughter Katrina's action for damages against Perth and Kinross Healthcare NHS Trust.

Jim Fairlie: his attempt to gain redress — actions i) and ii)

In 2004, Jim Fairlie felt compelled to abandon his action against the SWD after the judge advised, prior to the hearing,

> Even if Mr Fairlie proves what is averred (alleged) by him as fact in relation to that case, he has no claim in law on the basis either of duty of care or confidentiality.

Despite this set-back, in 2004, six years after he began his legal action in 1998, Jim Fairlie continued with his case against the NHS Trust, this being heard a month later, when the Judge, Lord Kingarth stated:

> It goes without saying that if, as Mr Fairlie claims, the psychiatrist made the diagnosis which it is said he did, and it was one reached carelessly and without proper investigation, his concern to seek redress is wholly understandable. I am nevertheless required to decide this case within the boundaries of the law as it has recently developed.

The action was denied, in part, on the basis that practitioners owe no duty of care to third parties.

Jim Fairlie writes:

> We knew that the third party duty of care position in law would be a problem but there had been a number of cases in recent law in England which encouraged me that things were changing. It had been established in the USA with the Gary Ramona case and in March of the year in which my case was thrown out there was a judgment in the Netherlands where a psychiatrist was found guilty of negligence and was forced to pay damages to the parents of one of his patients who had accused them after having gone through RMT (recovered memory therapy).

Daughter Katrina's action for compensation was summarised by Jim Fairlie:

> The case of Katrina Fairlie v Perth and Kinross Healthcare NHS Trust was due to go to the Court of Session in Edinburgh in March 2006 for a Day of Debate. In Scotland this is a day of legal argument to determine whether or not there is merit in allowing a case to go to proof.

Katrina's action for damages — action iii)

> Originally this date was fixed in March 2005, when the Day of Debate had to be postponed at the last minute because of a mistake in the legal papers presented to the Court. A few days before the hearing in March 2006, the Health Trust's legal team decided they would dispense with the Day of Debate and go straight to Proof. This meant that Katrina's case could not be struck out and, either the case would be heard in court or an offer would be made.

> Katrina had been told that it may be some time in 2007 before the case could be heard because of the complications of getting all sides to agree on a date. With the case postponed until 2007, it would be eleven years since the legal action was started and thirteen years since Katrina was first admitted to hospital with abdominal pains.

The NHS finally offered Katrina £10,000 which her QC strongly advised her to take. She refused and the NHS offered her £12,000, which the QC again advised her to take. The final offer of £20,000 was taken not because she was advised to take it but because her QC told her he would not appear for her if she refused it. As Katrina was on legal aid and having had an offer, there was no guarantee that the Legal Aid Board would sanction further representation and without it the case would be put back indefinitely. Fairlie's final bill was close to £200,000.

Jim Fairlie is writing a book on his experiences.

Part VII.

An international evil

32. An unwelcome export

'Hits' to the BFMS website from overseas (table 32.1), together with direct requests for help from individuals, and reports carried on the websites of BFMS sister organisations in other countries, show that the evil effect of false memories continues to spread across the world.

Not all countries where the phenomenon of therapy-induced false memories has taken root have the help of organisations such as the BFMS and FMSF (False Memory Syndrome Foundation) in Philadelphia with a full time staff supported by respected members of the professions. As Professor Chris French, Professor of Psychology at Goldsmiths, University of London, Member of the Professional and Scientific Advisory Board of the BFMS, and editor of the UK version of *The Skeptic* magazine, writing in *The Guardian* newspaper, said:

> Both (the BFMS and FMSF) have scientific and professional advisory boards to support them in their aims, which include providing support to those affected by such accusations, providing information and advice to professionals, and improving the understanding of false memories by encouraging and supporting academic and professional research [French, 2009].

Madeline Greenhalgh, Director of the BFMS, addressing the 2009 AGM and conference of the Society, said,

> Since the last AGM we have recorded case histories for about 50 new cases. People are more and more finding out about our work through the Internet and visiting our website ... Better still, is the opportunity to talk face-to-face and this is a service we have offered for anyone who asks if it is possible. One such couple, whom we met at the office, had travelled all the way from Norway — there was no one in their own country to turn to for help; they were able to have their questions answered and offered access to a vast archive of academic papers, newspaper and journal articles, reports, DVD and audio recordings and books. We are aware of organisations across the globe dealing with the problem and recently we have been in communication with a French group, exchanging ideas and learning about how they are handling cases. A considerable part of their workload relates to cults

due to a concern that during the process of indoctrination, pressure and influence are brought to bear on individuals, causing them to believe the worst of their families and to cut off all contact with them. Some of our members will identify with that process. A recent email was received from a forensic psychologist in Israel which noted that the country was new to the false memory phenomenon. Not good news.

Table 32.1.: Visits to the BFMS website

United Kingdom	1,696	(66)	Netherlands	14	(93)	Cyprus	5	(100)
United States	639	(90)	Greece	13	(92)	Egypt	5	(100)
Japan	152	(100)	New Zealand	13	(38)	Thailand	5	(100)
Australia	69	(86)	Philippines	10	(90)	Spain	4	(100)
Canada	69	(97)	Brazil	10	(100)	Italy	4	(100)
India	59	(19)	Malaysia	8	(100)	Indonesia	4	(25)
Ireland	40	(88)	Sweden	7	(86)	Portugal	4	(100)
France	29	(90)	South Africa	6	(100)	China	4	(100)
Germany	22	(86)	Switzerland	6	(67)	Croatia	4	(100)
Norway	18	(67)	Singapore	6	(100)	And another 35 countries		
Hong Kong	18	(67)	Sri Lanka	6	(33)			

* these figures are a sample/snapshot taken from Google Analytics

Overseas False Memory Societies

USA False Memory Syndrome Foundation — www.fmsfonline.org

Australia The Australian False Memory Association — www.afma.asn.au

New Zealand Casualties of False Sexual Allegations — www.geocities.com/newcosanz

France Alerte Faux Souvenirs Induits — www.psyfmfrance.fr

Germany Schulterschluss bei Sektenbetroffenheit e.V. based in Wuppertal, Germany has a subgroup Arbeitskreis Induzierte Erinnerungen (false memories) http://www.schulterschluss.info/index.php?id=50

Netherlands Werkgroep Fictieve Herinneringen — www.werkgroepwfh.nl

Sweden Forum for Families against False Incest Memories — www.enigma.se/info/FFI.htm

Notes

Content notes (page xxi)

1. In many cases that were not proceeded with by the police or Crown Prosecution Service, the accused were arrested and held for questioning in police cells, before being released. However, the nightmare for those falsely accused did not end there; months or years might elapse before the police or CPS informed the accused that they were not to be charged. Nevertheless, they sometimes remain under suspicion by social services and, in cases involving family members, the children being taken into care and parental access denied or restricted.

2. Referring to the book, *The courage to heal* in a Parliamentary debate (19 June 2003), MP Claire Curtis-Thomas, Chair of the All Party Group on Abuse Investigations said that many responsible psychiatrists and therapists regard the book 'as one of the most potentially damaging self-help books ever written. Its authors encourage readers to search their memories for dark and shameful episodes of sexual abuse which, they are told, may have been completely hidden by repression.'

   Dr James Le Fanu, writing in the *Sunday Telegraph* [2005], said of the book,

   > Its insights include the claim that "if you think you were abused, and your life shows the symptoms, then you were". It also encourages so-called survivors of recovered memory syndrome to engage in "pleasurable fantasies of murder and castration against those who have hurt them so terribly" (I kid you not).

   The courage to heal was listed as recommended reading in a proposed Scottish Executive publication, *Yes you can! Working with survivors of sexual childhood abuse* [Nelson and Hampson, 2005] which claimed that without 'higher qualifications and lengthy training,' thousands of people 'including staff and volunteers working in mental health, community projects, counselling and support services, health and social work services, homeless projects, addiction services, criminal justice, older people's projects and in young people's services' can recognise in adults symptoms of childhood sexual abuse. A group of eminent psychiatrists and psychologists raised objections to the booklet and it was withdrawn. An amended second edition including a section on "'Recovered' and 'false' memories" and without any reference to *The courage to heal* was published in 2008.

The courage to heal was also included in the 'Books on Prescription' scheme being introduced by a number of libraries. This, too, has led to objections from a group of professionals resulting in its withdrawal by some library authorities.

3. The terms 'recovered memory therapy' and 'regression therapy' are viewed with increasing scepticism. As a consequence practitioners have devised a number of alternatives. They include: 'traumatology' (signs of trauma in the past), 'traumatic amnesia', 'dissociation' or 'disconnection', 'Dissociative Identity Disorder' (DID) formerly known as 'Multiple Personality Disorder' (MPD), 'dissociated trauma', 'dissociative amnesia' 'age regression' or 'reawakening memories' and 'body memories.'

4. 'Recovered Memories of childhood sexual abuse: implications for clinical practice' [Brandon et al., 1998] (generally known as the 'Brandon' Report) was commissioned in May 1995 by the Royal College of Psychiatrists to

   a. enquire into reports made by adults, usually but not exclusively arising within a therapeutic relationship, of recovered memories of long-forgotten childhood sexual abuse, and

   b. to provide guidance for British psychiatrists in this difficult area.

Copies of the report may be obtained from the BFMS. The recommendations on duty of care may be found on pages 304–305. In 2006 the RCP announced the formation of a further working group to revisit the subject of memory but the chairman later withdrew and, as at time of publication, a successor had not been announced. A summary of the British Psychological Society's report, *Guidelines on memory and the law* [2008], is given in chapter 7.

5. From 1 July 2009, the Health Professions Council (HPC) assumed responsibility for considering allegations about fitness to practise of applied psychologists. Failure by the GMC and HPC to properly investigate complaints against their members and, if necessary, take appropriate disciplinary action, may result in their decisions being referred for review to the courts by the Council for Healthcare Regulatory Excellence (see CHRE website, 'Reviewing fitness to practise decisions under section 29'). Practitioner psychologists were included in the remit of the HPC and CHRE in 2009. The HPC has recommended that

it takes over the regulation of therapists and counsellors (see chapter 8 for further details).

The case heard by the BPS (chapter 30) pre-dates this change. Full details of the new arrangements for the regulation of applied psychologists may be found on the websites of the HPC and BPS.

6. Accusers who want to renew contact with their families on the condition the problem is never discussed are known as 'returners'. Those who accept fully and openly that their allegations were false are known as 'retractors'. The experiences of several retractors are related in Part 1.

Phoebe's story: 'Behind closed doors' (page 5)

1. Gillick competence is a term originating in England and is used in medical law to decide whether a child (16 years or younger) is able to consent to his or her own medical treatment, without the need for parental permission or knowledge. The standard is based on a decision of the House of Lords in the case *Gillick v West Norfolk and Wisbech Area Health Authority* [1985].

Louise's story: a story of real and false traumatic memories (page 21)

1. A 'pagan witchcraft tradition' (www.bbc.co.uk/religion/religions/paganism/subdivisions/wicca.shtml).

2. Katharine Mair's description in chapter 6 of attending a conference organised by Ritual Abuse Information Network (RAINS) describes the culture in which social workers, therapists and others come to believe in the widespread existence of satanic cults.

The regulation of psychotherapy (page 51)

1.

> Any final decision about whether psychotherapists and counsellors should become regulated is one for the Government and subject to parliamentary approval. If agreed, we currently anticipate that the earliest date the Register for psychotherapists and counsellors might open is 2011.

However, the legislative timetable is often subject to delay. Any decision about regulating a new profession is one for government and is subject to parliamentary approval, currently in Westminster and the Scottish parliament [Health Professions Council, 2009a, FAQ 19].

2. These include Practitioner Psychologists (9 Protected Titles and 7 Modalities), Arts Therapists, Occupational Therapists, Speech and Language Therapists and Paramedics. 'Aspirant' groups include Dance Movement Therapists. A full list of present and aspiring professions may be obtained from the HPC website www.hpc-uk.org.

A parent's view: the Kafkaesque world of 'recovered memories' (page 55)

1. Playwright Arnold Wesker was able to achieve a remarkable degree of understanding of the plight of falsely accused parents in his play *Denial*, premiered at the Bristol Old Vic. The play was based on lengthy, recorded interviews with victims families and depicts accurately the effects on the family and the progressive and insidious nature of the mind-control exercised by the daughter's therapist. A video of the play may be obtained from www.heritagetheatre.com.

2. Consultant gynaecologist and forensic medical examiner Dr Mary Pillai conducted a survey of outcomes of 22 families who became subject to criminal or civil proceedings when a female (some 90% of accusers in cases reported to the BFMS are women) adolescent or young adult developed a mental health problem.

> The resultant outcomes were mostly disastrous for the young person and the family. In every case there was no evidence supporting the allegations of abuse and substantive evidence they were false, yet this crucial information had not been sought [Pillai, 2002].

A survey of BFMS members by Professor Gisli Gudjonsson of the Institute of Psychiatry, London spoke of the 'horrendous consequences' of false allegations: 'I thought of taking my own life,' 'Family life completely disrupted,' 'Lost my only daughter and cannot talk about it,' 'The accused father died grief-stricken,' 'The accuser now completely separates herself from her family,' 'I have spent six years in prison without parole,' 'We have had to move to a new area and make new friends,' 'Complete breakdown of close family,' 'I'm unable to see my grandchildren,' 'I completely lost my confidence,' 'I have lost my career.'

A follow-up survey in 2003 recorded 'greater police involvement' with 'legal proceedings being instigated' [Gudjonsson, 2006].

A barrister's view: rights, risks and responsibilities (page 61)

1. Elizabeth F Loftus, Ph.D, is Distinguished Professor of Psychology and Law at the University of California, Irvine. She specialises in the study of human memory as applied to the field of law. She is widely published and the author of the book *Eyewitness testimony* [1979] and co-author of the book *The myth of repressed memory* [Loftus and Ketcham, 1994].

2. This quotation has been slightly edited from the original to reflect the wording and numbering of the most recent version of the Code for Crown Prosecutors.

3. *Daubert v Merrell Dow Pharmaceuticals Inc* (1993) 509 US 579

A solicitor's view: can symptoms be evidence? (page 71)

1. Obsessive Compulsive Disorder: Information is available on line from www.nhs.uk/conditions/obsessive-compulsive-disorder/Pages/ Introduction.aspx, www.ocduk.org/, http://www.nice.org.uk/CG031 and from many other websites.

Introduction to Part IV (page 85)

1. This was the figure in April 2010 and covered a 17 year period since the BFMS's inception in 1993. It represents approximately one-quarter of the total number of false memory cases reported to the Society.

Phillip Coates: successful appeal against Court Martial conviction for rape (2007) (page 103)

1. In response to a National Institute for Health and Clinical Excellence (NICE) report that all Post Traumatic Stress Disorder (PTSD) sufferers from PTSD should be offered a course of trauma-focused psychological treatment (trauma-focused cognitive behavioural therapy or EMDR), a critique of their recommendations was published by James Ost [2005]. A summary of this paper stated: 'The scientific response confirmed that it was akin to a placebo with no evidence basis for the treatment. It was described as having parallels with Mesmerism and a variant of traditional exposure therapy where the eye movements appear to be unnecessary. Some proponents of the technique believe the procedure can unlock traumatic memories' [Greenhalgh, 2005].

R v *Bowman* : unsuccessful appeal in 2006 against conviction in 2002 (page 113)

1. *Wednesbury unreasonable* is a legal term that, briefly, refers to a 'decision or reasoning' that 'no reasonable person acting reasonably could have made.'

Bibliography

News: Conduct Committee progress. *Newsletter of the British False Memory Society*, March 2008. 16(1):3.

Mr & Mrs A. Legal forum: comments on the Eastgate case. *Newsletter of the British False Memory Society*, 12(1):25–27, June 2004.

Ray Aldridge-Morris. *Multiple personality: an exercise in deception.* Lawrence Erlbaum, Hove, 1989. ISBN 0 86377 128 9.

American Psychiatric Association. *Diagnostic and statistical manual of mental disorders.* American Psychiatric Association, Arlington VA, third edition, 1980. ISBN 0 89042 041 6.

Ellen Bass and Laura Davis. *The courage to heal: a guide for women survivors of child sexual abuse.* Perennial, New York, 1988. ISBN 0 06 055105 4.

Janet Boakes. Legal forum: the role of the expert witness. *Newsletter of the British False Memory Society*, 13(2):13–15, October 2005.

Charles J Brainerd and Valerie F Reyna, editors. *The science of false memory.* Oxford University Press, Oxford, 2005. ISBN 978 0 19 515405 4.

Norman Brand, editor. *Fractured families: the untold anguish of the falsely accused.* BFMS, Bath, 2007. ISBN 978 0 9555184 0 9.

Sydney Brandon, Janet Boakes, D Glaser, and R Green. Recovered memories of childhood sexual abuse: implications for clinical practice. *British Journal of Psychiatry*, 172:296–307, April 1998.

British Psychological Society. *Guidelines for psychologists working with clients in contexts in which issues related to recovered memories may arise.* British Psychological Society, Leicester, June 2000.

British Psychological Society. Disciplinary notice: *Mrs Janet Sinclair. The Psychologist*, 20(12):753, December 2007.

British Psychological Society Research Board. *Guidelines on memory and the law: recommendations from the scientific study of human memory.* British Psychological Society, Leicester, June 2008. ISBN 978 1 85433 473 2. A report from the Research Board.

British Psychological Society Research Board. *Guidelines on memory and the law: recommendations from the scientific study of human memory.* British Psychological Society, Leicester, revised edition, April 2010. ISBN 978 1 85433 473 2. A report from the Research Board.

William Burgoyne. *Counselling or quackery? a personal view of the therapy industry and the therapy culture that underpins it.* Publish and be Damned, London, second edition, 2005. ISBN 1 905059 51 5.

William Burgoyne. Special focus: taking a closer look at R v *Thomas Bowman* and R v X. *Newsletter of the British False Memory Society*, 14(1): 2–7, September 2006.

Terence W Campbell. *Smoke and mirrors: the devastating effect of false sexual abuse claims.* Insight, New York/London, 1998. ISBN 0 306 45984 1.

Stephen J Ceci and Maggie Bruck. *Jeopardy in the courtroom: a scientific analysis of children's testimony.* American Psychological Association, Washington DC, 1995. ISBN 1 557 98282 1.

S Cook. Opening Pandora's box. In Adah Sachs and Graeme Galton, editors, *Forensic aspects of dissociative identity disorder*, pages 155–166. Karnac, London, 2008. ISBN 978 1 85575 596 3.

Frederick Campbell Crews. *The memory wars: Freud's legacy in dispute.* New York Review of Books, New York, 1995. ISBN 0 940322 04 8.

Crown Prosecution Service. *Code for Crown Prosecutors.* Crown Prosecution Service, London, 2010.

Tana Dineen. *Manufacturing victims: what the psychology industry is doing to people.* Constable, London, second edition, 1999. ISBN 0 09 479790 0.

Colin Feltham, editor. *Controversies in psychotherapy and counselling.* Sage, London, 1999. ISBN 0 7619 5640 9.

Christopher C French. Families are still living the nightmare of false memories of sexual abuse. *The Guardian*, 8 April 2009.

Pamela Freyd. News forum: letter from America. *Newsletter of the British False Memory Society*, 15(1):8–10, March 2007.

Madeline Greenhalgh. Editorial. *Newsletter of the British False Memory Society*, 13(1):1–2, February 2005.

Madeline Greenhalgh. Editorial. *Newsletter of the British False Memory Society*, 11(1):1–2, December 2009.

Gisli Gudjonsson. Family survey update. Paper presented to the AGM of the British False Memory Society, London, 25 March 2006.

Health Professions Council. Frequently asked questions on the statutory regulation of psychotherapists and counsellors. 2009a.

Health Professions Council. HPC publishes conclusions on the proposed statutory regulation of psychotherapists and counsellors. http://www.hpc-uk.org/mediaandevents/pressreleases/index.asp?id=405, 10 December 2009b. Press release.

Health Professions Council. Position statement: regulation of psychotherapists and counsellors. http://www.hpc-uk.org/mediaandevents/statements/psychotherapistscounsellors/, 10 December 2009c.

Health Professions Council. The statutory regulation of psychotherapists and counsellors. Report of the Psychotherapists and Counsellors Professional Liaison Group (PLG) incorporating recommendations to the HPC Council, 2009d.

Inquiry into the Removal of Children from Orkney in February 1991. *Report of the Inquiry into the Removal of Children from Orkney in February 1991: return to an Address of the Honourable the House of Commons dated 27 October 1992 [James J. Clyde].* Her Majesty's Stationery Office, Edinburgh, 1992. ISBN 978 0 10 219593 4.

John F Kihlstrom. Trauma and memory revisited. Paper presented at the 6th Tsukuba International Conference on Memory: *Memory and emotion*, 15 March 2005.

John F Kihlstrom. Trauma and memory revisited. In Bob Uttl, Nobuo Ohta, and Amy L Siegenthaler, editors, *Memory and emotions: interdisciplinary perspectives*, chapter 12, pages 259–291. Blackwell, Malden MA/Oxford, 2006. ISBN 978 1 405 13981 6.

Jean Sybil La Fontaine. *The extent and nature of organised and ritual abuse: research findings.* Her Majesty's Stationery Office, London, 1994. ISBN 0 11 321797 8.

Jean Sybil La Fontaine. *Speak of the devil: tales of satanic abuse in contemporary England.* Cambridge University Press, Cambridge, 1997. ISBN 0 521 62082 1.

James Le Fanu. In sickness and in health: the Church finds a false god in therapy. *The Telegraph*, 31 January 2005.

Elizabeth F Loftus. *Eyewitness testimony.* Harvard University Press, London, 1979. ISBN 0 674 28775 4.

Elizabeth F Loftus and Katherine Ketcham. *The myth of repressed memory: false memories and allegations of sexual abuse.* St Martin's Press, New York, 1994. ISBN 0 312 11454 0.

Elizabeth F Loftus and Laura A Rosenwald. Buried memories — shattered lives. *American Bar Association Journal,* 79:70–73, November 1993.

Richard J McNally. *Remembering trauma.* Harvard University Press, London, 2003. ISBN 0 674 01082 5.

Richard J McNally. The science and folklore of traumatic amnesia. *Clinical Psychology: Science and Practice,* 11(1):29–33, March 2004.

Richard J McNally. Debunking myths about trauma and memory. *Canadian Journal of Psychiatry,* 50(13):817–822, November 2005.

H Merskey. The manufacture of personalities: the production of multiple personality disorder. *British Journal of Psychiatry,* 160:327–340, 1992.

Alison Miller. Recognising and treating survivors of abuse by organised criminal gangs. In Randy Noblitt and Pamela Perskin Noblitt, editors, *Ritual abuse in the twenty-first century: psychological, forensic, social, and political considerations,* chapter 17. Robert D Reed, Bandon OR, 2008. ISBN 978 1 934759 12 7.

Peter Naish. Louise: a story of real and false traumatic memories. *Newsletter of the British False Memory Society,* 13(2):5–6, October 2005.

Sarah Nelson and Sue Hampson, editors. *Yes you can! Working with survivors of childhood sexual abuse.* Scottish Executive, Edinburgh, 2005.

Sarah Nelson and Sue Hampson, editors. *Yes you can! Working with survivors of childhood sexual abuse.* Scottish Executive, Edinburgh, second edition, 2008. ISBN 978 0 7559 5615 9.

Randy Noblitt and Pamela Perskin Noblitt. Redefining the language of ritual abuse and the politics that dictate it. In Randy Noblitt and Pamela Perskin Noblitt, editors, *Ritual abuse in the twenty-first century: psychological, forensic, social, and political considerations,* chapter 2. Robert D Reed, Bandon OR, 2008. ISBN 978 1 934759 12 7.

Richard Ofshe and Ethan Watters. *Making monsters: false memories, psychotherapy and sexual hysteria.* Charles Scribner's Sons, London, 1994. ISBN 0 684 19698 0.

James Ost. EMDR: of limited use, whichever way you look at it. *Health Watch Newsletter*, 58:4–5, 2005.

Mark Pendergrast. *Victims of memory: incest accusations and shattered lives*. Upper Acess Books, Hinesburg VT, second edition, 1996. ISBN 0 942679 18 0.

Mary Pillai. Allegations of abuse: the need for responsible practice. *Medicine, Science and the Law*, 42(2):149–159, April 2002.

Harrison G Jr Pope. *Psychology astray: fallacies in studies of "repressed memory" and childhood trauma*. Upton Books, Boca Raton FL, 1997. ISBN 978 0 89777 149 8.

Harrison G Jr Pope and James I Hudson. Can memories of childhood sexual abuse be repressed? *Psychological Medicine*, 25(1):121–126, January 1995.

Harrison G Jr Pope, P S Oliva, and James I Hudson. Scientific status of research on repressed memories. In D L Faigman, D H Kaye, M J Saks, and J Sanders, editors, *Modern scientific evidence: the law and science of expert testimony (Volume 1, Pocket Part)*, pages 110–155. West Law Publishing, St Paul MN, 2000.

Carl Raschke. The politics of the "False memory" controversy: the making of an academic urban legend. In Randy Noblitt and Pamela Perskin Noblitt, editors, *Ritual abuse in the twenty-first century: psychological, forensic, social, and political considerations*, chapter 6. Robert D Reed, Bandon OR, 2008. ISBN 978 1 934759 12 7.

C A Ross. Epidemiology of multiple personality disorder and dissociation. *Psychiatric Clinics of North America*, 14(3):503–517, September 1991.

Royal College of Psychiatrists' Working Group on Reported Recovered Memories of Child Sexual Abuse. Reported recovered memories of child sexual abuse: recommendations for good practice and implications for training, continuing professional development and research. *Psychiatric Bulletin*, 21(10):663–665, October 1997.

Carol Rutz, Thorsten Becker, Bettina Overcamp, and Wanda Karriker. Exploring commonalities reported by adult survivors of extreme abuse: preliminary empirical findings. In Randy Noblitt and Pamela Perskin Noblitt, editors, *Ritual abuse in the twenty-first century: psychological, forensic, social, and political considerations*, chapter 3. Robert D Reed, Bandon OR, 2008. ISBN 978 1 934759 12 7.

Karl Sabbagh. *Remembering our childhood: how memory betrays us*. Oxford University Press, Oxford, 2009. ISBN 978 0 19 921840 0.

Flora Rheta Schreiber. *Sybil*. Regnery, Chicago, 1973. ISBN 0 80920 001 5.

Robert Shaw. Obituaries: Geroge Davison: an appreciation. *Newsletter of the British False Memory Society*, 16(1):19–20, March 2008.

Michelle Smith and Lawrence Pazder. *Michelle remembers*. Congdon & Lattes, New York, 1980.

The Telegraph. Obituary: Lord Clyde. *The Telegraph*, pages 664–670, 13 March 2009.

Jeffrey S Victor. *Satanic panic: the creation of a contemporary legend*. Open Court, Chicago, 1993. ISBN 0 81269 191 1.

Rosie Waterhouse. Satanic inquisitors from the town hall. *The Independent on Sunday*, 7 October 1990a.

Rosie Waterhouse. Satanic cults: how the hysteria swept Britain. *The Independent on Sunday*, page 3, 16 September 1990b.

Richard Webster. *Why Freud was wrong: sin, science and psychoanalysis*. Harper Collins, London, 1995. ISBN 0 00 255568 9.

Daniel B Wright, James Ost, and Christopher C French. Recovered and false memories. *The Psychologist*, 19(6):352–355, June 2006a.

Daniel B Wright, James Ost, and Christopher C French. Research: ten years after — what we know now that we didn't know then about recovered and false memories. *Newsletter of the British False Memory Society*, 14(1): 8–14, September 2006b. Extended version of D B Wright, J Ost and C C French 'Recovered and false memories' *The Psychologist 19*(6):352–355 June 2006.

Michael D Yapko. *Suggestions of abuse: true and false memories of childhood sexual trauma*. Simon & Schuster, London, 1994. ISBN 0 671 87431 4.

Index

Lightning Source UK Ltd.
Milton Keynes UK
03 December 2010

163803UK00002B/12/P